Recruiting and Managing Volunteers in Museum and Other Nonprofit Organizations

AMERICAN ASSOCIATION for STATE and LOCAL HISTORY

AMERICAN ASSOCIATION FOR STATE AND LOCAL HISTORY BOOK SERIES

ABOUT THE SERIES

The American Association for State and Local History Book Series addresses issues critical to the field of state and local history through interpretive, intellectual, scholarly, and educational texts. To submit a proposal or manuscript to the series, please request proposal guidelines from AASLH headquarters: AASLH Editorial Board, 2021 21st Ave. South, Suite 320, Nashville, Tennessee 37212. Telephone: (615) 320-3203. Website: www.aaslh.org.

ABOUT THE ORGANIZATION

The American Association for State and Local History (AASLH) is a national history membership association headquartered in Nashville, Tennessee, that provides leadership and support for its members who preserve and interpret state and local history in order to make the past more meaningful to all people. AASLH members are leaders in preserving, researching, and interpreting traces of the American past to connect the people, thoughts, and events of yesterday with the creative memories and abiding concerns of people, communities, and our nation today. In addition to sponsorship of this book series, AASLH publishes *History News* magazine, a newsletter, technical leaflets and reports, and other materials; confers prizes and awards in recognition of outstanding achievement in the field; supports a broad education program and other activities designed to help members work more effectively; and advocates on behalf of the discipline of history. To join AASLH, go to www.aaslh.org or contact Membership Services, AASLH, 2021 21st Ave. South, Suite 320, Nashville, TN 37212.

Recruiting and Managing Volunteers in Museums and Other Nonprofit Organizations

A Handbook for Volunteer Management

Second Edition

Kristy Van Hoven and Loni Wellman

ROWMAN & LITTLEFIELD
Lanham • Boulder • New York • London

Published by Rowman & Littlefield
An imprint of The Rowman & Littlefield Publishing Group, Inc.
4501 Forbes Boulevard, Suite 200, Lanham, Maryland 20706
www.rowman.com

86-90 Paul Street, London EC2A 4NE

British Library Cataloguing in Publication Information Available

Library of Congress Cataloging-in-Publication Data

Names: Van Hoven, Kristy, 1983- author. | Wellman, Loni, 1981- author. | American Association for State and Local History.
Title: Recruiting and managing volunteers in museums and other nonprofit organizations : a handbook for volunteer management / Kristy Van Hoven and Loni Wellman.
Other titles: Recruiting and managing volunteers in museums | Handbook for volunteer management
Description: Second edition. | Lanham : Rowman & Littlefield, [2024] | Series: American Association for State and Local History book series | Original title: Recruiting and managing volunteers in museums: a handbook for volunteer management. | Includes bibliographical references and index. | Summary: "Recruiting and Managing Volunteers in Museums is back with a highly anticipated second edition! A decade after the first edition's release, this updated handbook offers fresh insights into the world of museum volunteers and their vital contributions to the success of organizations, both big and small"-- Provided by publisher.
Identifiers: LCCN 2024026476 (print) | LCCN 2024026477 (ebook) | ISBN 9781538187630 (cloth ; alk. paper) | ISBN 9781538187647 (paper ; alk. paper) | ISBN 9781538187654 (electronic)
Subjects: LCSH: Volunteer workers in museums--Handbooks, manuals, etc. | Museums--Management--Handbooks, manuals, etc. | Nonprofit organizations--Management--Handbooks, manuals, etc.
Classification: LCC AM121 .V45 2024 (print) | LCC AM121 (ebook) | DDC 069/.63--dc23/eng/20240614
LC record available at https://lccn.loc.gov/2024026476
LC ebook record available at https://lccn.loc.gov/2024026477

♾️™ The paper used in this publication meets the minimum requirements of American National Standard for Information Sciences—Permanence of Paper for Printed Library Materials, ANSI/NISO Z39.48-1992.

Contents

Preface

Since we started this project in 2013, we have strived to pull together helpful strategies, resources, and examples to help volunteer coordinators build and maintain stellar programs at their organizations. When we started drafting the first edition of *Recruiting and Managing Museum Volunteers*, we knew there was a gap in publications that provided comprehensive, well-rounded, and easily implementable steps for creating and running a volunteer program. What we did not realize was how many volunteer coordinators felt that they were alone on an island trying to figure all this stuff out on their own. Over the last ten years we have learned that together, as a network of volunteer coordinators, supervisors, and museum leaders, we can provide inspiration and support to each other. And that we all have the opportunity to see our organizations grow into thriving gathering places at the heart of the communities we serve, all with the help of our passionate volunteer corps.

Experience, passion, and new energy are just some of the intangible things volunteers bring to an organization. For many museums and galleries, volunteers are crucial contributors to the financial and operational stability of the organizations with which they are associated. Volunteers provide much-needed support for tours, special events, on-site and off-site programs, and administration. Through engaging projects, regular communication, and ongoing recognition for a job well done, you can build meaningful long-term relationships with your volunteers and community. Over time, volunteering fosters more engagement at museums and allows for stronger relationships between museum staff, supporters, members, and donors. Building a healthy, vibrant volunteer program will ensure the long-term health and sustainability of any nonprofit organization.

Museums, galleries, research institutions, zoos, as well as other nonprofits, recruit volunteers of all ages and experiences to help with a variety of projects both on-site, throughout the community, and through virtual experiences. From hosting events, programs, and guiding visitors, to working alongside a curator or exhibition designer, to office filing, fundraising, and other administrative activities, there are a number of roles for volunteers in any organization. Offering opportunities to use a volunteer's talents and knowledge or providing a unique project that allows a volunteer to learn or experience new things, is one of the greatest rewards a museum can offer their volunteer.

The work of a volunteer can range from special events to routine daily tasks. Special projects are a great way to introduce people to your organization, its mission, and day-to-day work. Both routine and long-term projects allow volunteers to feel invested. Engaging in long-term projects provides your volunteers with the opportunities to cultivate lifelong relationships with the museum or gallery, the staff, and fellow volunteers. These connections often create a sense of a second family for many volunteers. On the other hand, routine projects allow volunteers to help "run" their favorite museum. Understanding your volunteers, their motivations, and their needs will lead to a successful volunteer management program.

As volunteer coordinators, we started this project by asking ourselves some questions about volunteers and how they fit into our institutions. Drawing on our background in museum programming, volunteer management, and community engagement, we started reflecting on some questions that are commonly asked by museum leadership and our colleagues embarking on a volunteer program of their own: Where does one start in developing a volunteer department or program? How can I find the talent I need for my projects or program? What can I do to support and nurture my volunteers? What happens when a volunteer is unable to follow through on their commitment? What should a museum do if a volunteer leaves your institution under less-than-favorable conditions? These questions are just the beginning, and more are likely to arise during any development process, program management, and especially during volunteer and project evaluations. However, with a bit of guidance, any institution can create a great volunteer management program

Volunteers create a sense of community through their roles at the museum.
Image courtesy of the authors.

that both supports the institution's mission and fulfills each volunteer's needs and expectations.

This book was written for you, the volunteer coordinator, as well as museum staff, and organizational leadership. We will provide tips, tricks, and examples of volunteer management programs and scenarios that will help guide museum and gallery staff to build a flourishing volunteer program. The best-laid plans often require flexibility, and these chapters allow you to pick and choose information and strategies that are most helpful to your institution. This book is broken down into eight chapters to help you quickly address needs and potential issues as they arise, and we hope they will be referenced often.

The first chapter introduces volunteers, in general, and what we have learned from the changing landscape of volunteerism in the past ten years. Our basic questions remain from our original edition, however: Who are our volunteers? What motivates them to return or join organizations in the new decades of the twenty-first century? What will the landscape look like for volunteering in a post-pandemic world? We will identify what volunteers mean to museums and what the next decade holds for volunteers in general. Volunteers can bring so much to an organization; we will explore all the traditional roles as well as the new roles volunteers can take on in today's museums and galleries. We are also aware of the fact that community demographics are in flux. Over the next decade, communities will continue to shift, leading to new challenges and successes as communities work to redefine themselves. We will examine how various demographics can bring their unique experiences to your organization and how a diverse volunteer program will provide stability for the future of the organization.

In the second chapter, we will explore how crucial it is to consider diversity, equality, inclusivity, and accessibility in the sustainability of your volunteer program. We will identify the major demographics that make up a majority of museum volunteers. From retired professionals to students to the growing pool of virtual volunteers, we will review demographics that will bring a variety of expertise and services to museums and galleries now and into the future. We will also address the needs, motivations, and types of projects that are best suited for each volunteer demographic, as not all volunteers are created equal. The last section of the book will include fictional scenarios that illustrate the principles addressed in each section. These scenarios will assist you in strategizing on how to effectively recruit, train, and retain volunteers within each of the identified groups. Keep in mind there may be more special interest groups than those we have identified, but this section will provide insights and raise questions that will be helpful when evaluating the diversity of your volunteer groups.

The third chapter charts a path for you, or other museum leaders, to create a sustainable volunteer program. It also provides guidance on how to reimagine existing volunteer programs to support new initiatives and goals for the museum field. Additionally, it explores how your volunteer program can adapt and align with the changes in your community. Finally, we will look at how you can support volunteers through their journey at the museum, from first introductions, through exploring projects to celebrating a job well done. Chapter 3 will set you up to make educated decisions to support and build your program with confidence.

Chapter 4 will guide readers in developing policies, procedures, and forms for new or existing volunteer programs. This chapter includes sample material from forms and policies to other items that may be helpful when developing a volunteer program. Items such as internal request forms, volunteer job advertisements, project outlines, time management forms, and evaluations and recognition tips will help you and your volunteers to stay on the same page and have a wonderful experience moving the museum's mission forward. The samples in this section are generic in nature and should be used as a guide in creating your own site-specific forms and procedures. Having specific documents that reflect the museum's needs and institutional policies will encourage volunteers to feel like a part of the organization and help the volunteers know they are held to the same standards as other museum staff. This feeling will help build a strong team consisting of leadership, staff, and volunteers.

Communication and community building are cornerstones to a successful volunteer program.
Image courtesy of the authors.

Chapter 5 will help you start the crucial conversations around volunteers who might need a bit more assistance in order to be successful in their role. Conversely, we will touch on how to celebrate a job well done. Volunteers have life cycles, just as many other relationships in our professional and personal lives. In this chapter, we will help you understand how to identify volunteers who may be struggling to fulfill their commitment to the museum, and how to compassionately support the volunteer through their life cycle at the museum. We will also introduce conflict resolution techniques and how to foster a volunteer's graceful exit from the project, department, or museum if necessary. Although we are all mindful of the gift of time volunteers give us, it is also okay to recognize that sometimes that gift is no longer supporting the organization positively. It is okay—we will repeat, it is okay—to discuss exit strategies with volunteers, just as you would a staff person. This chapter explores various ways to celebrate your volunteer team and offers strategies for troubleshooting and finding success by making small adjustments. It provides insights on how to turn a negative situation into a productive and supportive experience. This chapter best serves as your guide to support conversations with volunteers, staff, and leadership when a crucial crossroads presents itself.

The next section of chapters is in response to a series of questions we have had since the release of the first edition of *Recruiting and Managing Museums*. Fundraising has become a job for everyone, and many volunteers have asked their coordinators (who have in turn asked us), "What can I do to help?" We know that fundraising is hard and not for the faint of heart. This chapter will explore opportunities for volunteers to get involved in your fundraising initiatives. We will provide you with some suggestions and guidance on how to manage expectations and set your volunteers up for fundraising successes as you partner with the development and philanthropy teams.

The second chapter in this section also tackles some common questions we have received over the last decade: How can I facilitate increased involvement of the board in my museum? What is the role of a volunteer board? And how can volunteer-led organizations be sustainable and successful community partners? This chapter will highlight ways you can support board activities and museum leadership in ensuring the board is working toward the mission and vision of the museum in a way that supports and respects the other stakeholders in the organization. This is not a comprehensive chapter, but rather an introduction to inspire further training and research into board relationships for nonprofit professionals.

Our final chapter will merge the ideas, principles, and tips introduced in the book with applicable, real-life scenarios. The case studies will explore issues that volunteer managers and their volunteers face daily. Each study will examine a different museum as well as volunteers from different demographics. The cases are designed to help you make connections between the lessons in the book and real-life applications that you will deal with day to day. Through the review of volunteer groups, their motivations, and special site considerations, you will be able to develop a concept for your organization's volunteer department.

This publication is designed to be used in its entirety as an introduction to volunteer management and sustainability, or it can be used in parts to strengthen areas in an already established volunteer department. With our experiences in volunteer coordination, project management, and nonprofit leadership, and a sampling of documents we use in our institutions, you will have the tools necessary to develop a world-class volunteer program for your museum.

We hope that this book becomes an invaluable resource for you. By establishing a solid foundation that draws inspiration from your colleagues, and incorporating valuable insights gained from past experiences, you can begin to construct a framework for your programs. This framework will enable you to cultivate a diverse, inclusive, and supportive network of museum volunteers, managers, and leaders that will ensure that organizations big and small are able to support and fulfill their mission.

Acknowledgments

We would like to extend our heartfelt gratitude to all those who have supported us in the creation of the second edition of *Recruiting and Managing Volunteers in Museums and Other Nonprofit Organizations: A Handbook for Volunteer Management*. This new edition aims to not only update core philosophies about supporting successful volunteer teams but also to delve into the vital topic of building a volunteer corps that prioritizes diversity, inclusion, and accessibility in every aspect of nonprofit and museum practice. We are grateful for the opportunity to recognize and explore the ways in which inclusion and equity can be integrated into volunteer programs and encourage you to explore how you can make each volunteer opportunity accessible to any volunteer who wishes to help your organization.

Additionally, we are excited to delve into the "New Era" of volunteer management, as well as touch upon the delicate subject of working with volunteer boards and how to connect with volunteers who are keen to help with fundraising and sustainability efforts. Rest assured, we will never advocate for volunteers to be the sole fundraisers for a nonprofit when there are opportunities for staff to lead those initiatives, but rather, we will explore the ways in which the relationships with volunteers can drive fundraising efforts in a tasteful manner that respects their contributions to the organization and prevents them from questioning their own dedication. As we embark on this journey, we are eager to continue our exploration of volunteers, volunteer management, and museums in a post-pandemic world.

To our family, friends, colleagues, and the team at Rowman & Littlefield and AASLH, thank you for continuing this important journey with us.

—Kristy Van Hoven and Loni Wellman

Part I

The Ins and Outs of a Great Volunteer Program

1

Reflections on the Past Ten Years

VOLUNTEER TRENDS AND THE TWENTY-FIRST-CENTURY
MUSEUM EXPERIENCE

WHY A SECOND EDITION? WHY NOW?

This is not a book about COVID-19. We do not want this book to be about COVID-19. We are trying very hard not to write COVID, but three sentences in, we have used it three times. There is no doubt that the world has changed in the last five years, not to mention the changes in the last ten. Political and social changes, environmental and economic changes, reimagining what work is for each of us, a lot has changed, and it changed rapidly. And yet, we found there is still a lack of comprehensive writing for volunteer managers in the nonprofit and charitable sectors, and specifically in museum settings. As we turn to new adventures and new challenges as a field, it makes sense that we update *Recruiting and Managing Volunteers in Museums: A Handbook for Volunteer Management* now. Blink, and we will have to update again.

In addition to addressing the evolving landscape of volunteer management, we will continue to emphasize the importance of building and maintaining strong relationships with volunteers. In this second edition, we want to expand the invitation to participate in dialog around volunteering with our colleagues across the nonprofit landscape, and although we primarily focus this book around museum experiences, any organization that utilizes volunteers or hopes to build a volunteer team can take principles, sample documents, and even some scenarios and transplant them into any setting where a volunteer works.

Volunteers are the lifeblood of museums and nonprofit organizations and a direct connection to the community each organization serves. Volunteer programs will be the most successful community engagement program your organization will ever have. A volunteer corps's dedication and passion are crucial to the success and stability of any organization. Strong relationships between volunteers and their coordinators are at the heart of a strong volunteer corps. We will delve into strategies for recruiting, training, and retaining volunteers, as well as techniques for recognizing and rewarding their contributions. If you take one thing away from this publication, it will be understanding that the bond between you and each of your volunteers, and the bond they have with each other, is the essential ingredient to success.

One significant change in this second edition is the increased recognition of the value of diversity, equity, inclusion, and accessibility (DEIA) in volunteer programs. We now understand that creating a welcoming and inclusive environment is not just a moral imperative or a social responsibility, but there is also a strategic advantage to bringing the best people into your organization and keeping them for the long term.

In this edition, our goal is to give you a starting point to assess your own volunteer program and the DEIA initiatives that will strengthen your team and organization. As we explore ways that volunteer programs can reflect the diversity of your community, it is essential that you honestly look at your volunteer corps and dig deeper. Here we will only scratch the surface. It is essential to recognize that this publication is not the appropriate platform to fully unpack the implications of systemic racism, gender identity challenges, management theory, or engaging in the debate about interns and compensation. Each of these topics deserves much more ink and paper. We simply want to give you the tools needed to dig below the surface level of buzzwords and go beyond

Creating lasting bonds with volunteers helps build a sustainable volunteer program.
Image courtesy of the authors.

"checking a box." We will explore ways to ensure that your volunteer programs reflect the diversity of your community and provide opportunities for an array of individuals to engage and contribute.

Another important aspect to consider is the increasing reliance on technology in volunteer management. The past decade has seen significant advancements in volunteer management software, online platforms, and virtual volunteering opportunities. Each year volunteers become more and more savvy with technology available to them in everyday life. Museums like other charities can rely on the fact that the volunteer corps is becoming more technologically proficient before they enter the museum. We will explore some of the new technologies and provide guidance on how to leverage them effectively to streamline processes, improve communication, and enhance the volunteer experience.

As we reflect on the changes that have occurred over the past ten years, we are also mindful of the enduring principles that still hold true in volunteer management. The importance of clear communication, thoughtful planning, ongoing evaluation, and regular recognition of a job well done cannot be overstated.[1] These foundational elements remain essential for successful volunteer programs, regardless of the external factors that may influence the field.

Throughout this second edition, we will draw on the expertise and experiences of volunteer managers from museums of all sizes and types. We believe that sharing diverse perspectives and real-world examples is crucial for providing a comprehensive and practical guide to volunteer management. We are grateful to all the individuals and organizations who have contributed their insights and case studies to this edition.

The second edition of *Recruiting and Managing Volunteers in Museums and Other Nonprofit Organizations: A Handbook for Volunteer Management* aims to provide a comprehensive and up-to-date resource for you, the volunteer coordinators in the museum field. We also hope that museum leaders and volunteer coordinators in other types of nonprofits can benefit from the discussion contained within these pages. While much has changed in the past decade, we remain committed to the timeless principles of effective volunteer engagement and management. We hope that this book will serve as a valuable tool for both novice and seasoned volunteer coordinators alike, as you navigate the ever-changing landscape of volunteerism in museums.

WHO ARE MUSEUM VOLUNTEERS?

Since the dawn of the cabinets of curiosity, museums and galleries have depended on the goodwill of others to develop collections, promote ideas, and foster civic pride. Early museums usually consisted of rooms or galleries in private estates and universities. The exhibitions at these early museums featured exotic specimens mounted behind glass in awe-inspiring poses, and galleries of carved stones and marbles from ancient lands. Visitors wandered the galleries gazing into foreign places with a sense of wonderment and childish excitement for the world outside. Patrons of these early museum collections traveled regularly to new and faraway lands and acquired exquisite objects during their journeys. Upon their return home, patrons installed their newly acquired treasures in their museums. These exotic objects helped promote a family's standing within society, as it was through their gallery patronage that the society would know the family's wealth and value.

By the nineteenth century, museums transitioned from exclusive status symbols into larger, public institutions. Their doors were opened to all types of visitors from scholars and students to working-class families. Museums and galleries shifted their focus from gathering general curiosities to scientific collecting and from casual visitors to public education. Through this shift, museums and galleries became centerpieces of their communities. The vast galleries became alive with tours and lectures. Visitors would travel to museums to learn about science, history, and the arts from expert curators and trained docents. Museum staff told the tales of ancient civilizations and helped visitors explore the natural world around them. Masters and students of the arts would come to the museum galleries to practice their crafts, while an eager public watched them create their masterpieces.

By the dawn of the twentieth century, museums were hubs of community activity. They continued to reach out to their communities by developing special weekend programs and civic celebrations. As these programs became popular, community members were drawn to museums and galleries looking to become involved and support their local museums. Mission statements and exhibit plans became an important part of gallery development and interpretive

Jan Brueghel the Elder and Peter Paul Rubens, 'Sight' (1617)
Image courtesy of Museo del Prado, Madrid via Wikimedia Commons, Public Domain.

planning, and, as a result, they opened up the world of the professional museum curator and administrator. Museum staff quickly recognized the need for a robust and dedicated volunteer force to help with the day-to-day operations of the museum. Volunteers became pivotal to the success of tours, gallery programs, and visitor services. Museum administrators also recognized the value of volunteers assisting with special projects, such as exhibit construction, special event planning, and marketing projects.

"Friends of" and other auxiliary groups quickly emerged as additional communities of support for museums and galleries. The mission of these groups was to help cultivate community interest and museum support. Auxiliary groups joined like-minded individuals to provide financial support and manpower for a variety of projects. Many of these auxiliary groups worked like an exclusive club. Members would be recruited and expected to pay dues to the group, join working groups, and promote volunteer opportunities for their organization. The groups tended to recruit new members who excelled in skills that would benefit the organization. For museums, these auxiliary corps were proficient at organizing and training docents who provided general museum gallery tours and programs, as well as organizing and serving as hosts for special events. Through their extensive social networks, auxiliary groups were able to cultivate additional financial support and collection pieces for their museum or gallery in addition to connecting with the public in the galleries and museum spaces.

"Friends of" groups emerged as civil advocates, and they promoted museum missions within their communities. These groups were often less exclusive and allowed anyone willing and able to pay the membership dues to join. Members were also expected to be active participants in the group's activities. In addition to directly working with the museum on special projects and events, these groups organized their own fundraising campaigns to support projects and initiatives in the museum. By the mid-twentieth century, auxiliary groups were leading fundraisers and were the number one source for museum volunteers.

Noting the increased importance and activity of volunteers, museums created volunteer coordinator positions and developed departments dedicated to volunteer management in the late twentieth century. The American Association for Museum Volunteers published its Standards and Best Practices for Museum Volunteer Programs in 2011. In it, they outlined the importance of a volunteer coordinator by stating that a museum or gallery must ensure "that the volunteer program has staff support and resources needed for its success."[2] It also stated that each museum or gallery must have at least one dedicated paid employee responsible for managing or coordinating the volunteer program.

Volunteer coordinators worked with auxiliary groups to provide support for a variety of museum activities, to foster community interest in the museum, and to align missions and activities between the auxiliary groups and their museum. Volunteer coordinators also took on the management of interns and

Auxiliary groups of volunteers continue to be strong partners in museum operations.

Image courtesy of Friends of the National Museum of the American Latino, X.

students, as well as other volunteers such as scout groups and civic clubs. Today, volunteer coordinators (or those who wear the volunteer coordinator hat on occasion) oversee the vast majority of museum volunteer activities across all museum departments and activities, while auxiliary groups work closely with museum leadership on development, special projects, and events.

Today's volunteers represent all segments and demographics of the community. In any healthy volunteer group, you will find high school and college students, professionals, retirees, and corporate volunteers. Students who apply for volunteer positions are looking to fulfill community service requirements for classes. University and graduate students seek out volunteer opportunities to develop skills necessary for the job market, while professionals look to broaden their skills through unique volunteer opportunities. Retirees have traditionally been the largest group of museum and gallery volunteers, mostly because traditionally museums have been open during weekdays, and retirees had the most flexibility in their schedule; however, what was once a tradition is now changing and evolving with the museums and work culture in recent years.

While most retirees look for opportunities to engage with others socially and give back to their communities in meaningful ways, other volunteers may come to the museum with different motivations. Volunteers who come to your museum in a group bring a collective spirit of camaraderie and purpose. These groups may include civic clubs like the Rotary, Masons, Scouts, or corporate teams from local and national businesses. Their motivation is clear: they want to utilize the group volunteer opportunity to team build while also contributing to local institutions that culturally align with their own mission. Each type of volunteer—whether from a corporate background, a community organization, or a youth group—brings a unique and diverse experience to your volunteer corps. Their combined skills, perspectives, and enthusiasm means they are ready to tackle any project that comes their way. By harnessing their collective energy, museums can achieve more, engage the community effectively, and create lasting impact.

THE MUSEUM VOLUNTEER OF THE FUTURE

According to the "Museums and Society 2034: Trends and Potential Futures" report from the Center for the Future of Museums (CFM), "museums will take the lead in reshaping civic involvement" through their collections, programs, and community outreach.[3] Throughout their history, museums and galleries have been a place for people to come together to learn, socialize, and get involved in civic discourse. In the twentieth century, museums and galleries shifted their focus from displaying collections to developing interpretive strategies and formal learning opportunities, which in turn developed a huge need for volunteer docents, educators, and volunteers who could provide a variety of visitor services.

During the late twentieth century, museums started opening up their collections and access to curators and archivists, allowing for more volunteer opportunities in the "back of house." Looking toward the future, museums will continue to be places of community gathering and education. There is a drive for museums to be community hubs that bring collections, stories, experiences, education, and well-being together and foster crucial conversations that lead to growth and inclusion in the community.

As well as providing new and exciting volunteer opportunities through virtual and digital engagement, museums as a place are essential partners in civic development and well-being. Essentially, museums are moving "from an inward concentration on their collections to a newly articulated outward concentration on various publics and communities that they serve[d]" (Anderson 2004); as more museums enter the conversation on engagement, and champion voices that have yet to be heard, and work together to make history, art, science, culture, and technology accessible, they will continue to grow into active hubs of learning and storytelling across communities.

With the general population becoming more diverse, museums will continue to grow in their role as places for cultural exchange. The Center for the Future of Museums predicts there will be major demographic changes in museum visitorship and staff by 2034. With the shift to greater ethnic diversity in communities surrounding museums, it will fall to curators, educators, and museum volunteers to develop and implement exhibits, programs, and other outreach activities that reflect the museum's or gallery's growing community diversity. This trend is being realized across the country with the opening and planning of community museums that explore and celebrate the cultural diversity of their communities. Museums such as the Peralta Hacienda Historical Park in Oakland provide tours and programs that appeal to their local communities.

Communities are proud to support and participate in museums that address issues such as racial division and historical struggles, as well as those that celebrate a rich melding of cultures, heritage, and contributions to the local society. Other groups, like the Smithsonian Institution, have spent years growing their collections to represent the growing diversity throughout the United States; as their collections have grown, they have developed independent museums that reflect important cultural identities that have contributed immensely to the history of this country. Other museums have grown out of commemorations for historic people or places that changed the course of history and bring to light hidden and lesser-known stories to illustrate the diversity

Museums create space for communities to come together.
Image courtesy of Peralta Hacienda Center for History and Community, Facebook.

of the country and its local communities. Regardless of the topics covered, museums and galleries will continue to foster diversity among their collections, staff, volunteers, and community in the years to come.

Along with the change, gender roles in our communities are evolving at an exhilarating pace. No longer bound by rigid traditional norms, individuals now chart their own courses, unafraid to pursue passions and forge unique paths. This metamorphosis extends beyond individual lives—it redefines the very concept of "family." Families, like the vibrant brushstrokes of your favorite painting, come in myriad forms: nuclear, extended, chosen, blended. They weave together rich narratives, each thread contributing to the vibrant fabric of our society. And within this intricate weave, museums find a treasure trove. Volunteers, representing these diverse family structures, breathe life into exhibits, infusing them with personal stories, cultural nuances, and shared experiences. Museums, and nonprofit organizations in general, then become living and breathing reflections of our multifaceted world.

Economic changes are also taking place in communities around the world. More households currently rely on multiple incomes to sustain their family's needs and priorities. For many, employment and leisure time focus has moved toward personal fulfillment and the ability to contribute to society in ways that align with personal values, strengths, and aspirations. It is this freedom of choice and the recognition of diverse contributions that truly shape today's workforce.

The concept of family is also evolving to accommodate the diverse needs and values of each member. This shift in family structures is prevalent across every community. The Center for the Future of Museums reports that gender and parenting roles will continue to evolve in the future, leading to a wider range of family definitions that make up any one community. It is important for museums to acknowledge and adapt to these changes, considering how families spend their leisure time, engage with their community, and organize their priorities. By understanding the varied composition of families and their evolving roles, museums can effectively shape their operations around community needs and cultivate a diverse and representative volunteer corps.

Each of these unique family makeups affects their communities and the institutions providing services to the community. Grandparents may have more time to shuttle children to various activities, including school, summer camps, and weekend events. Students and some working adults may have time to attend special lunchtime or early morning tours and lectures. Of the adults who may not be available for weekday programs, many are able to attend events in the evening. Understanding the gender and generation roles in your community will help drive museum programming and exhibitions, highlight potential areas for volunteer opportunities, as well as highlight those demographics most likely to commit to volunteer projects at a museum, art gallery, or other community cultural institution.

Many students will turn to museums and other nonprofits as a way to help engage in their community while learning and honing skills necessary for their careers. Skills in business, marketing, and project management will be high among employer's wish lists, and museums and galleries can foster learning opportunities that will prepare students for roles in business, education, and civil service while benefiting from the students' work.

Museums, galleries, and zoos as well as other nonprofits like patient support groups, animal shelters, and community welfare organizations will also develop lifelong relationships with volunteers through their early volunteer experiences. Individuals who have volunteered with nonprofits early in their lives are more likely to continue volunteering and supporting those organizations as they progress professionally. These early career and student volunteers become lifelong donors of time and money, as well as huge advocates for the organization and its mission over time. According to the Fidelity Charitable Gift Fund's Volunteerism and Charitable Giving in 2009 Executive Summary, "[V]olunteers donate ten times more money to charities than those who do not volunteer." On average, those who did not volunteer in the last twelve months donated only $230 a year to charity, while volunteers donated $2,593 a year. Of those who volunteered, 67 percent claimed that they donated money to the same charities where they volunteered.[4]

Technology is growing and developing at a rapid rate, a trend that is expected to continue. For museums and galleries, this can be a scary thought, as technology growth usually leads to more expensive, yet necessary, pieces of equipment. Nevertheless, museums and galleries can benefit greatly from technological advancements in many areas. Developments in technology are making the on-site gallery space more visible to a global audience and more accessible to visitors and volunteers around the world. People with physical and geographic limitations are now able to visit museums large and small through virtual tours, museum apps, webinars, and other digital outreach programs. Museums are opening their doors to a new type of visitor and subsequently a new type of volunteer, and, as technology continues to develop, museums and galleries will be able to reach an even larger audience through digital engagement.

Using video conference calls, group chat rooms, social media, and digital online databases, museums can partake in recruiting more diverse volunteers that may be beyond their local traditional volunteer pool and develop innovative ways to engage their volunteers more deeply in their collections and programs. A quick internet search gives the potential volunteer a number of digital volunteer options, including "back-of-house" tasks such as artifact identification and cataloging, program development, and online chats and lectures.

Among the most popular projects in museums are cataloging and transcription projects. Digital copies of documents and recorded oral histories are posted online to be transcribed by volunteers through controlled-access workspaces. Museums around the world are using closed websites to catalog archival material such as research logs, travel journals, and transcribed oral histories, which can then be uploaded or linked to a collection database or research software used in the museum and archives.

Other museums are posting collections on open-access sites such as Flickr and asking for the public's help in identifying and tagging collection pieces and historic photographs. Although it may be scary to ask for help from anyone, most museums have reported receiving many great contributions that have helped open the collections to new audiences, as well as inspired new ways of exhibiting pieces that appeal to a larger community. Public projects such as these allow potential volunteers to try volunteering without committing to a specific project and the training that the project may require. Open-access volunteer opportunities can be a museum's first step toward recruiting and weeding out potential long-term volunteers. Regardless of the type of activity, museum cataloging and artifact identification projects have always been a staple in the list of volunteer opportunities. With more technology, we are, for the first time, able to take these opportunities out of the back rooms and curatorial centers of museums and place them front and center in the eyes of the public.

Another emerging area of digital engagement is educational programming. Museums and galleries are taking their visitors out into the field with archaeologists and biologists. Curators can live stream visits to various museums and collection storehouses, bringing the visitor on a behind-the-scenes tour of museums across the world. Educators and program facilitators can develop online courses and lectures that bring participants up close to works of art and artifacts they would otherwise view from afar (if they were able to view them at all).

So how can volunteers assist with these types of projects? Traditionally, the volunteer's roles in programs have been the extra hands that provide assistance to visitors or serve as way-finders and crowd control. Digital program volunteers assist in these projects by providing research for collection items that are slated for use in the program, or by serving as the museum's technical support in the galleries where they help connect those in the field or "on assignment" to the visitors in the museum. Volunteers can provide guidance to areas around the museum and perhaps even provide context during the online chats or offer tours of the museum that help connect visitors to the collection on a deeper level. Some volunteers prove themselves as subject matter experts and may serve the museum best by providing digital tours and lectures on behalf of the institution. No matter the program, digital engagement will continue to become an important outreach tool for any institution, which will continue to open new doors to the museum for visitors and volunteers.

Museums have a responsibility to their communities to provide educational and entertaining opportunities for engagement in culture, history, the arts, and sciences, but museums and galleries operate on a limited budget that

Technology in the volunteer experience is on the rise.
Image courtesy of the authors.

seems to be shrinking just as more demands are being placed on the institution and its staff. The Center for the Future of Museums reports that budgets and funding will continue to be an issue moving into the future. Growing demands on finite financial resources will require everyone to look for ways to increase engagement while maintaining a stagnant, if not shrinking, bottom line.

In this realm of community service, volunteers can be "worth their weight in gold" by providing exceptional museum visits and programs, connecting with local advocacy groups, and reaching out to their extensive social networks to promote the museum's mission, programs, and development campaigns. Volunteers will encourage others in their community to participate in the museum through passionate and emotional appeals that reflect their personal experiences. These personal appeals help connect people to each other and the institution on a personal level, which will serve the museum well in future projects and recruitment campaigns.

However, the most valuable role for passionate volunteers can be during an institution's marketing and development campaign. When a volunteer shares their experiences with others, they do so in a heartfelt and genuine manner. Passionate volunteers will donate time and money to causes they are proud of and believe have a future both in their personal lives and in their community. They will challenge others—their friends, family, and other community members—to join the cause as well. Through drives, matching grant programs, and personal appeals, development campaigns that involve volunteers tend to yield more returns than a campaign purely driven by the staff or an outside development firm while costing the institution very little in resources or cash.

Volunteers now and into the future will prove to be one of the more valuable resources a museum can have. A healthy and robust volunteer force will ensure the museum or gallery's success in programs and community engagement, as well as a stable financial base to support day-to-day operations and special events. In many cases, the casual volunteer will develop a lifelong passion for advocacy, which results in long-term volunteer service and connections for future community and financial development opportunities. Above all, volunteers recognize the importance of their role in shaping the future of the museum. With an understanding of the current trends and an eye for the future, volunteers, their coordinators, and museum leadership will form an essential support team for museums and galleries in the years to come.

NOTES

1. Geesje Duursma et al., 2023, "The Role of Volunteers in Creating Hospitality: Insights from Museums," *Journal of Hospitality and Tourism Management* 54: 373–82.
2. American Association for Museum Volunteers, 2011, Standards and Best Practices for Museum Volunteer Programs.
3. American Alliance of Museums. Center for the Future of Museums (2008), "Museums and Society 2034: Trends and Potential Futures."
4. Fidelity Charitable Gift Fund, 2009, Fidelity Charitable Gift Fund Volunteerism and Charitable Giving in 2009 Executive Summary, http://www.fidelitycharitable.org/docs/Volunteerism-Charitable-Giving-2009-Executive-Summary.pdf.

2

We Need You!

The world is a wonderfully diverse place with new ways and opportunities to become engaged. Opportunities are exciting but sometimes challenging. Museums have pivoted from stalwart centers of knowledge to active hubs that bring together the local and global communities. Museums weave together the communities' stories in a robust narrative of our connections and relationships to each other and the world around us. As we move beyond the confines of the COVID-19 pandemic era, we have encountered fresh challenges and exciting opportunities to make museums and their collections resonate with all members of our community and extend beyond those directly involved as active stakeholders in the mission and programs.

Museums are facing new challenges to visitorship, development, environmental sustainability, programming, and collections management. You may be asking yourself *How can we stay relevant to our community? Can we lessen our negative impact on the environment? How can we provide the support our community expects from us? Can we provide a safe place for people to come together to confront the challenges they face? How can we engage in exciting and supportive ways with the world around us?*

Often when the word *volunteer* is used, an image comes to mind for us all. It may be a parent helper on school field trips or a nice retired professional who tells stories to visitors as they pass through a room in a historic home. For some, it may be a young adult who is cleaning up the activities after a day with young campers, or an intern who is typing away at a spreadsheet in the office. But aren't those still the faces of museum volunteers? The answer is maybe, but that is not all.

Today museums struggle with answering the question *Who are our volunteers?* Or maybe more accurately for some, *Where are our volunteers? Or how do we ignite volunteers to join us?* The relevance of volunteering is often coming into question for museum leadership and community members at large. With so many activities vying for time, attention, and funding, do people really want to share their time and expertise with an organization? And without compensation? In this chapter we will explore the relevance of volunteerism today, what motivates and inhibits volunteers connecting with your organization, and what considerations are required to have a successful foundation on which to build (or rebuild) an active and robust volunteer program. By understanding the changing demographics in the volunteer landscape, you and any volunteer coordinator can identify opportunities to effectively utilize volunteers to further your organization's mission, both within your community and beyond.[1]

MOTIVATIONS OF MUSEUM VOLUNTEERS

Today's museum volunteers can be summed up as invested. They are deeply invested in the organizations in which they choose to serve. Their passion and dedication drive them to contribute their time, knowledge, and energy to your organization. Whether it is guiding visitors through exhibits, cataloging artifacts, or organizing events, these volunteers play a vital role in enriching our programs and engaging our communities. Their commitment ensures that museums remain vibrant and accessible spaces for all. Volunteers seek opportunities where they can align themselves with an organization's mission, vision, programs, and community impact. They look for organizations that routinely demonstrate their investment in activities and values that are important to the volunteer. When developing or reimagining your organization's volunteer program, it is crucial to remain mission-driven and focused on the impact each volunteer can have on your organization and community.

The concept of volunteerism has evolved beyond the act of lending a helping hand. Volunteers in modern museums are motivated by a desire to contribute in a meaningful way to the organization's objectives, explore their interests, and further build their standing among peers and community members. Volunteers bring with them a wealth of skills, expertise, trustworthiness, and passion. This makes them valuable assets to any museum. Recognizing this, it is essential for you and your museum leadership to design and manage volunteer programs that harness and nurture each volunteer's investment.

A mission-driven volunteer program that is purposefully designed is one that aligns with the overarching values and goals of the museum. This coincides with the desire of today's volunteers to be involved and invested in their museums. Your volunteer programs should clearly communicate how volunteers can actively contribute to the museum's mission and vision and make an impact within their larger community. By outlining the specific tasks and projects available, your volunteers can understand how their efforts will contribute to your organization's success and make the museum accessible through their contributions. This clarity of purpose not only attracts committed volunteers but also ensures that their time and skills are utilized effectively and efficiently.

Today's volunteer represents their community and the causes they are passionate about.

Image courtesy of Alina Vozna, Wikimedia Commons.

Representation is a crucial aspect of creating an inclusive museum experience and volunteer program. It is important to acknowledge the significance of Diversity, Equity, Inclusion, and Accessibility (DEIA) in shaping a meaningful museum experience for all. When organizations embrace strategies to focus on DEIA, they signal their commitment to fostering a more equitable and welcoming environment. But why are volunteers particularly interested in working with such organizations, and why is it essential to focus on these initiatives? Volunteers are drawn to organizations that align with their values. When an organization actively promotes DEIA, it resonates with individuals who believe in and stand for fairness, justice, and equal opportunities. Many volunteers have personal experiences related to diversity, equity, or accessibility. They may have faced barriers themselves or witnessed others struggling due to lack of representation. By volunteering with an organization that prioritizes DEIA, they may feel connected to a cause that matters deeply to them.

Volunteers recognize that museums are no longer exclusive ivory towers. They have evolved into community hubs where diverse voices can and should be amplified. By participating in DEIA efforts, volunteers actively contribute to making these spaces more inclusive, welcoming, and reflective of the communities they serve. Engaging with DEIA initiatives provides volunteers with insights into different cultures, histories, and perspectives. It broadens their understanding and enriches their own lives.

Volunteers expect organizations to walk the talk. When DEIA practices are embedded in both public-facing programs and behind-the-scenes operations, it demonstrates an authentic commitment. It is not just about ticking boxes; it is about creating a museum experience that reflects the richness of humanity. Volunteers play a pivotal role in this journey, and their passion drives positive change. Now is the time to assess how well your volunteer program is keeping up with this responsibility.

AN INCLUSIVE MUSEUM

In order to make museums welcoming for all, it is necessary to create an environment where everyone feels comfortable, included, and represented in the museum experience. To achieve inclusivity, it is essential to reflect on personal experiences where you have felt unfamiliar and uncomfortable. By taking a moment to ask yourself questions to aid in understanding the challenges and concerns experienced by your visitors, volunteers, and staff, you can gain valuable insight and create change that makes all of your stakeholders feel more welcomed and included in the museum. As a volunteer coordinator, you will need to evaluate the roles and opportunities created for volunteers. Do the positions allow your volunteers to be their true selves while participating in their museum role? Do each of your volunteers and staff members support and respect the backgrounds, stories, and lived experiences of their volunteer colleagues? Does your museum explore topics or present programs that may be hurtful or exclusionary to volunteers or their lived experiences?

Your volunteers are a representation of the community your museum serves and hopes to serve in the future. Understanding your volunteers through their experiences and learning how they engage with the museum helps bridge knowledge gaps, misunderstandings, or feelings that make one feel excluded (however unintentionally). Allowing for open and accepting dialog between you and your volunteers is a crucial step in creating a successful volunteer program. It is through this communication that ideas can be shared, concerns can be addressed, and improvements can be made. You should encourage everyone to actively participate in conversations, listen to each other's perspectives, and respond thoughtfully and respectfully. By fostering an environment of open dialog, you will be able to collectively work toward the betterment of the volunteer program while continuing to find further opportunities to incorporate DEIA into everyday practice.

CREATING EQUAL OPPORTUNITIES

Creating opportunities for all volunteers involves actively seeking out and engaging individuals from diverse backgrounds. This requires reaching out to underrepresented communities, partnering with local organizations, and implementing targeted recruitment strategies. By widening the scope of outreach efforts, museums can attract a more diverse range of volunteers while fostering an inclusive and representative environment.

Modifying your current volunteer opportunities with the goal of becoming more inclusive involves reevaluating existing roles, responsibilities, and expectations. It is critical that volunteers from different backgrounds have the opportunity to actively contribute their unique perspectives and expertise. This may involve providing training and support to staff and volunteers, encouraging them to share their insights, and actively incorporating their ideas into the museum's programs and initiatives.

Encouraging leadership to reflect your museum's community among the staff and board is another important step you can take in creating an inclusive volunteer program. This can be achieved through intentional recruitment practices that prioritize building a team with diverse experiences and stories to bring to the organization. It is essential for museum leadership to represent the diversity of the community it serves and hopes to serve in the future. Having a board, leadership team, staff, and volunteer team that represents the larger community that surrounds the organization will create confidence across the wider public in the strategic decisions and operational goals at your museum.

As volunteer coordinators, it is your responsibility to advocate for the needs of current and potential volunteers across departments at the museum. By actively engaging in discussions around DEIA, you can contribute to the ongoing development and improvement of the museum's volunteer program. This may involve collaborating with other departments, initiating training programs, and implementing policies that prioritize accessibility and representation in each of the department's strategic directives and day-to-day work. Creating an inclusive space requires intentional efforts to ensure that all individuals feel welcomed and valued. By reflecting on personal experiences, creating diverse volunteer opportunities, modifying existing roles, and influencing staff and board composition, you can begin to foster an environment where everyone contributes and thrives. As a volunteer coordinator, you play a vital role in advocating for inclusivity and should actively engage in promoting DEIA within your organization, not just the volunteer program.

ACCESSIBLE VOLUNTEERING

From removing physical or technological barriers to participation to creating opportunities to engage with volunteer projects in unique and supportive ways, making an accessible museum volunteer experience can provide a unique challenge, but the rewards of overcoming such barriers to participation can lead to a wonderfully rich and robust experience for your volunteers, visitors, and museum community as a whole.

Traditionally the word accessibility has referenced overcoming the physical obstacles that prevent someone from participating in an activity. In recent years accessibility has grown in understanding to encompass mental, emotional, social, and technological barriers as well as physical ones. Museums are exploring new ways to actively engage a wider range of visitors and open more opportunities for volunteers through accessible experiences. When you are creating accessible opportunities for volunteers at a museum, it is important to understand your volunteer team's needs and the limitations of your museum's space, budget, policies, and other barriers that might exist. With a little bit of planning, you will find there are a lot of ways to integrate accessible experiences into your museum program that benefit volunteers, visitors, and staff alike without draining precious resources for the organization.

At the very least, the physical location where the volunteer will do their work needs to be accessible. For each volunteer, this may mean different things and it is important to take a moment to think through any barriers that may exist in their physical space. Be sure to include volunteers in the discussions, as they can be extremely insightful on issues that you may not be aware of, and how to overcome barriers to access that pose a challenge for them. Are there stairs or narrow hallways that the volunteer must navigate over the course of their duties? Is it easy to make a change to overcome those barriers? How about restroom or break room facilities, is it easy to navigate to those areas when needed? Are the doors all abilities friendly? Many libraries, archives, and collection rooms utilize tables with computers or other equipment. Are those friendly to those volunteers who use assistance devices? Is the volunteer opportunity inside or outside? If outside, are there accessible trails and walkways? Are there rest areas that are shaded or near to a building if need be?

Take a moment with each new project or opportunity to evaluate any physical challenges to participation and have a conversation with your volunteer(s) about any concerns they have about their physical working space. Open dialog will help make a volunteer feel appreciated and help prevent potential physical harm to volunteers and visitors on-site.

Another area where you should take a moment to evaluate accessibility needs is with technology and access to various technologies. If there is a silver lining to the last few years, it has been the increase in technological literacy. However, there are still challenges faced by some volunteers when it comes to their ability to access and successfully navigate technology. From using technology in the museum setting to having the appropriate access to technology to support remote volunteering opportunities, it is your job to make sure that necessary technology is available and accessible to volunteers. It is also important that your volunteers are comfortable using and troubleshooting the basics so that they are successful at their project.

An example might be using tablets at an event for ticket sales and donations. If a volunteer is set to sell and scan tickets or accept donations through

Providing hands-on training helps volunteers become familiar with their duties.
Image courtesy of John Fino.

an app at an event, make sure that your volunteer team knows how to navigate the basics of the tablet, how to complete transactions, what information is imperative to collect, and answering visitor questions while they complete the transactions. Or perhaps you have a team transcribing scanned historical documents at home or in the library room. Do your volunteers need to provide their own tablet or computer or will you be providing the hardware as part of the project? How about the software?

If your museum utilizes a special computer program in digitization projects or cataloging, make sure you are providing the software to the volunteer. Check that the volunteers know how to navigate between windows (scanned image and transcription document) and how to connect to the internet at home or in the museum. Are there special notes or functions a volunteer needs to know how to do? Can they highlight passages or make comments on an image or PDF?

Fully think through the project you are asking of your volunteer. You could create a tip sheet to help troubleshoot any technology issues that may arise for your volunteer. If you do not feel that you have the tools to create a basic cheat sheet, rely on your internal partners in the IT department, or find a more advanced staff member. Most importantly, if a project requires technology and/or a volunteer to use their own device/internet/software, make sure that requirements are listed in any job description so that the volunteer is aware of the technology needs required for the project.

The last area of accessibility we will explore briefly is the area of sensory and emotional accessibility. Museums can be delightfully busy and full of wonderful sights, sounds, and activity; but for some, that can be overwhelming. You may find that some volunteers prefer to have low-sensory experiences or a place where they are not confronting objects, images, or activities that may trigger negative memories or reactions for them. This can be a very difficult area to navigate as a volunteer coordinator, but it is important to recognize where some activities may be more emotionally or mentally challenging for some volunteers. It is important to build a positive relationship with each of your volunteers, actively building trust and maintaining open lines of communication so that when a volunteer encounters a challenge, they will be able to openly discuss with you ways that can move the museum forward.

Accessibility is an important consideration to keep at the forefront of your mind when planning a successful volunteer program. Understanding the needs and challenges a volunteer may face during their time with your organization will help build an empathetic and resilient volunteer corps that contributes to the long-term mission and goals of the organization in a really successful and positive way. Above all, make sure you take time to learn about your volunteers individually, and just like you would with coworkers, donors, and other stakeholders, take a moment to check in with each volunteer regularly and be ready to respond to needs and challenges when they are shared with you.

REPRESENTATION MATTERS

As with other areas of museum work, representation in the volunteer corps matters.[2] Finding ways to encourage community members to participate in your museum helps build trust and long-term relationships that can be a huge benefit to your organization over time. Developing a representative volunteer team and responding to the changing dynamics of a community can be a creative challenge; but highlighting the diversity of volunteers and their experiences will help promote a more robust, diverse, and effective volunteer team.

Evaluating diversity can be uncomfortable for some, with goals and reality often running in different directions. It is best to pull together a team that can help you evaluate your program and look for ways to provide more opportunities to engage more community members in your museum. Start your process by evaluating your volunteer team including all board members, special volunteers, and interns who may not report to you directly. How well does your team mirror community members and visitors? Check with those in your museum who are responsible for visitor studies and other community development organizations like tourism boards, city housing and zoning departments, and mayor and representative offices, as well as other community support organizations. In addition to understanding some key demographics about your community, you will build partnerships with community leaders who can help support your organization with future projects and initiatives too.

Step-by-Step Diversity Checklist:

- Evaluate community demographics and how well your organization reflects the community at large.
- Identify areas to increase representation to more closely align with the community and visitors.
- Connect with community leaders.
- Create adviser/working groups for special projects at your organization.
- Maintain active meetings/dialog through all project development and implementation.
- Identify ways to engage with program or exhibition development on an on-going basis.
- Create regular check-ins with volunteers, staff, leadership, and community stakeholders to maintain an active commitment to representing the community.

By taking time to evaluate and understand your community and visitors, you will help demonstrate your commitment to an inclusive, accessible, and supportive museum experience for everyone. Whether you are part of a small staff and take on the administration, exhibitions, programs, and collection management on your own, or if you are part of a larger organization where there are departments supporting each of the museum's activities and needs, it is important to make a case for any volunteer coordinator or volunteer department manager to join in the diversity, equality, inclusion, and accessibility conversations.

As the direct connection between the organization and the volunteers who serve in the museum, many of these initiatives may rest with you, and your input is a crucial voice representing current and future volunteers at the museum. Take time to deliberately include DEIA principles into your daily operations and you will find that very quickly the organization will feel a more welcoming environment for the whole museum community.

MUSEUM VOLUNTEERS: WHO ARE THEY AND WHAT MOTIVATES THEM?

ADULT VOLUNTEERS: OPPORTUNITIES THAT MAKE A DIFFERENCE

Adult volunteers, generally those between the ages of twenty-five and sixty-five, account for a large portion of a museum's volunteer force. A survey of international volunteers in arts and culture estimates that 50 percent or more of the arts and culture volunteer workforce are adults (ages thirty to sixty-five).[3] In this section, we will look at adult volunteers and their relationshipswith museums and nonprofit organizations, in addition to their needs when it comes to volunteering. Adult volunteers are defined as those volunteers who are out of school and working in a profession or maintaining a job and/or household. Adults generally have the ability to choose their activities and work out a schedule to accommodate their interests and commitments.

Adults choose activities and causes that reflect their values and the values they wish to see among their family and community. Their personal standings within their communities can also direct adults in choosing their volunteer roles. Many adults who are eager to volunteer at cultural and community organizations find that museums and galleries offer a prestigious and unique opportunity to get involved with their communities. They are able to utilize the professional skills acquired throughout their careers while also having the chance to learn new skills that support their career growth and development. Adult volunteers can be subject matter experts in topics covered in the museum and will lend expertise and authority to programs and publications. Adults, both those who are still active professionals and those who have retired, are great assets to your institution and can provide a variety of services.

Many adult volunteers have a passion for the charitable work they are involved in. They are willing to extend that involvement by serving on boards, chairing committees or working groups, and taking the lead on special projects. Adult volunteers contribute to museums and galleries through ambassador,

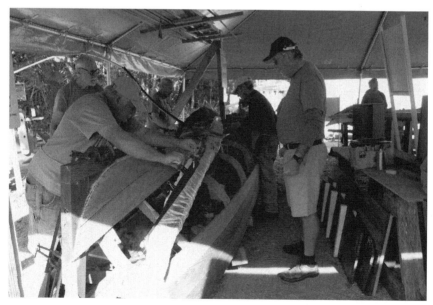

Corporate teams, groups of friends, or other new adult volunteers help get things done at any organization.
Image courtesy of authors.

friend, and advocate roles by using their extensive social networks. The ability of the adult volunteer to reach out to a comprehensive network of friends, family, and colleagues can serve a museum well during volunteer and donor cultivation activities, as well as promoting special programs and events. Inspiring adult volunteers to engage continuously with your museum or gallery is the biggest challenge faced with managing this group of volunteers.

Adult volunteers have a variety of motivations driving their desire to volunteer. In general, adults will volunteer with organizations that support a community's development and well-being. They will actively engage with an organization if they feel they are making a difference. According to one American Alliance of Museums survey,[4] museums drive economic development, education, and natural resource conservation in nearly every community, which increases the overall economic and physical health of local communities. Museum volunteers are attracted to specific positions due to their interests and how those interests align with the museum's mission or subject matter. Each volunteer is looking for a way to actively participate in an organization that shares their values and provides an opportunity to utilize talents or offer unique experiences to engage with their community.

COVID-19 has undoubtedly had a significant impact on adult volunteerism, both in terms of the number of volunteers and the hours they contribute. A study by Fidelity Charitable highlights some interesting trends in this regard.[5] It is encouraging to see that more than half of volunteers, approximately 53 percent, have reported that their volunteering time has remained unchanged. This demonstrates the resilience and dedication of individuals who continue to prioritize giving back to their communities and how important their investment in nonprofit organizations is, even in the face of a global pandemic.

What is particularly noteworthy is the 30 percent of volunteers who have actually increased their hours of service. There are several reasons for this positive trend. First, many individuals have felt a stronger urge to become more involved in social and community causes. The crisis has laid bare the vulnerabilities and inequalities in our societies, prompting people to take action and make a difference. Additionally, personal invitations or requests from friends, family, or organizations have played a role in inspiring individuals to increase their volunteerism and overall support for museums and galleries. Finally, the pandemic saw lots of folks retire early, while still wanting to contribute.

On the other hand, it is noted that 17 percent of volunteers have experienced a decrease in their volunteer time. This decline can be attributed to various factors, with changing priorities being the most common reason cited by 43 percent of these individuals. The pandemic has forced many people to reassess their priorities and focus on immediate concerns such as personal health, family, and financial stability. Consequently, some individuals may have had to reduce their volunteer commitments in order to address these pressing needs.

Regardless of their background and future plans, adult volunteers want to give to organizations that will benefit from their time. It is important to find out what the adult volunteer wants to gain from their time with your museum and match those needs to projects within the museum. It is okay to design and develop new projects to meet the needs of adult volunteers, as it is important to foster interest in new projects and allow the volunteer to take ownership of the project as soon as possible. It is not wise to keep adult volunteers waiting for projects. Adult volunteers are usually willing to work on small tasks or large projects so long as their time commitment can be flexible and accommodate any change in schedule and availability.

Adults, especially those with a professional background, will need measurable goals and outcomes. People like to be inspired by a project and know what milestones they need to reach to meet their goals. Even small projects need to have clearly stated goals and objectives; we have found it helpful to develop a checklist or outline of the project that the volunteers can keep with them to ensure they are progressing in the appropriate direction. A simple project task list will do the trick to keep all on task and mindful of next steps.

HISTORICAL POSTCARD PROJECT DIGITIZATION CHECKLIST FOR VOLUNTEERS

Objective: To digitize and preserve a recently acquired collection of four hundred historic postcards that were accessioned into the archival collection in 2023. This project will support the end goal of creating a digital exhibit that showcases the collection's historical and cultural significance to a wider audience and make images available for researchers in our collection management system.

Volunteers will report directly to the archives/collection manager during this project. The volunteer coordinator will assist when called upon.

This project is an on-site project, and technology assistance is available through the archives/collection manager.

- **Receive artifacts**:
  Goal: Receive a batch of postcards that have been identified by the archivist for digitization. Review processing plan and any special handling needs or digitization needs with staff.
  Milestone: Receive artifacts from the project manager.
- **Prepare artifacts**:
  Goal: Ensure postcards are ready for digitization.
  Milestone: All artifacts are properly handled, cleaned, and organized.
- **Set up equipment**:
  Goal: Ensure all necessary digitization equipment is functional and calibrated.
  Milestone: Equipment is set up and tested for proper functioning.

- **Digitize artifacts**:
  Goal: Digitize each item according to guidelines provided by staff. Ensure DPI, Color calibration, and digital storage location is in accordance with processing plan.
  Milestone: All artifacts are successfully digitized.
- **Review and edit images**:
  Goal: Ensure digitized images meet quality and accuracy standards.
  Milestone: All digitized images are reviewed and edited as needed.
- **Add metadata**:
  Goal: Add relevant metadata as outlined by the processing plan to each digitized image.
  Milestone: All digitized images have complete metadata.
- **Organize and store digitized images**:
  Goal: Properly organize and store digitized images to mirror physical processing of collection for easy intellectual tracking and digital access. Return physical objects to archives/collection manager.
  Milestone: All digitized images are organized and physical objects are stored in a secure location.
- **Submit batches to project manager**:
  Goal: Submit batches of digitized images and metadata to the collections manager.
  Milestone: Batches are submitted at specified milestones (e.g., monthly).
  Repeat steps above if multiple batches of material are submitted for digitization.
- **Address issues and concerns**:
  Goal: Promptly address any issues or concerns that arise during digitization.
  Milestone: All issues and concerns are communicated to the project manager and resolved.
- **Complete digitization and celebrate**:
  Goal: Successfully complete the digitization project.
  Milestone: All artifacts are digitized, and a celebration event is held to acknowledge volunteers' contributions.

TIMELINE

Month 1:

- Read the digitization project goals and objectives document.
- Familiarize yourself with the digitization workflow document provided by the collections manager.
- Attend the volunteer training session to learn proper artifact handling and digitization techniques.

- Practice with digitization equipment and workspace tools, including scanners, cameras, and image editing tools and collection database (metadata and digital storage).

Month 2:

- Begin digitizing artifacts according to the provided workflow document.
- Complete digitization of 100 postcards.

Month 3:

- Continue digitization process and ensure image quality and accuracy.
- Complete digitization of next batch of 100 postcards.
- Submit first batch of digitized images and metadata to collections manager.

Month 4:

- Address any issues or concerns encountered during the digitization process.
- Complete digitization of next 100 artifacts.
- Submit second batch of digitized images and metadata to the collections manager.

Month 5:

- Continue digitization process and maintain proper storage and handling procedures.
- Complete digitization of next 100 artifacts.
- Submit third batch of digitized images and metadata to the collections manager.

Month 6:

- Finalize digitization process and ensure all artifacts are properly documented.
- Complete digitization of remaining artifacts.
- Submit final batch of digitized images and metadata to the collections manager.
- Celebrate project completion with fellow volunteers.

An accompanying how-to guide for any technology or special deliverables will also help a volunteer be self-reliant. Take the following project, for instance: a small development department needs to have annual membership renewal letters sent out by the end of the week. The volunteer might need to pull the mailing list, generate labels, compile renewal packets, and stuff envelopes. Although the process may seem logical, it is worth taking the time to review all the steps with the volunteer and further mention how this project might impact the museum.

Creating excitement around a project allows the volunteer to feel more involved with the museum's activities, and their output quality will improve because they understand how the project fits into the bigger institutional picture. To help further encourage the volunteer during the project, volunteer supervisors should regularly check on the volunteer and his or her project. Asking about their progress or needs during the project will make the volunteer feel like a valued and supported member of the museum team. Ultimately, it is important for the volunteer's supervisor or manager to understand the unique needs of each of their adult volunteers and respond to those needs appropriately.

In the next five to ten years, the role of adult volunteers in nonprofit organizations will remain significant. As we move forward, more and more companies are increasing their corporate social responsibility initiatives and encouraging their employees to get involved in community service through sponsored volunteer programs. Some health insurance companies offer discounts to corporations, or individuals, who actively volunteer. These company-driven volunteers form a new group of adult volunteers who are motivated by company incentives to contribute to community groups. Museums and galleries can leverage their relationships with these companies by creating or customizing projects that align with the company's requirements for employee volunteer opportunities. By working closely with company-driven adult volunteers, museums can establish long-term partnerships with these companies, potentially leading to direct financial support or in-kind goods and services in addition to an ongoing volunteer force.

Adult volunteers will continue to embrace their social roles within organizations by actively participating in boards, committees, and auxiliary groups for museums and galleries. With more adults prioritizing their careers before starting families, adult volunteers will bring a wealth of professional training and skills to their volunteer positions, contributing to the growth and success of these organizations.

THE GOLDEN GENERATIONS: VOLUNTEERING AFTER SIXTY

In this section we will explore the volunteers over the age of sixty who may be nearing or through retirement, no longer have children living at home with them, and who have a bit more freedom day to day to engage in their passions and explore new opportunities to learn and engage in their communities.

Although usually identified as the "adult volunteer group" in volunteer surveys and reports, this volunteer group makes up another large portion of most museum and gallery volunteer teams. These volunteers live a more fluid and leisurely lifestyle, which involves frequent travel, local leisure activities (such as clubs and recreation league sports), and volunteering for a variety of organizations. They generally do not have dependent children or family members at home, but they might have long periods of absence from their volunteer positions, as they travel to see family or host their family a number of times throughout the year. Retired volunteers may choose to live in their communities on a seasonal basis, which can also lead to sporadic volunteer schedules.

Recently retired volunteers have a great deal of energy for projects and tend to give more hours on a regular basis than working adult volunteers or busy families. Older retired volunteers, however, may not have the stamina to work long shifts but might be interested in working short shifts multiple times a week. It is important for you as a volunteer coordinator to understand and adapt to limitations and needs that may arise with this group in order to ensure long-term success with the older volunteers.

Many museums and galleries are able to provide a space for generations to connect with each other, including opportunities for older volunteers to connect with others in their communities in impactful ways. Volunteers over the age of sixty enjoy active roles in museums such as being docents, program leaders, and special event volunteers. Many volunteers enjoy engaging with visitors on a social level and helping families, newcomers, and community members explore exhibits and galleries while sharing their stories and expertise. Program volunteers, who actively engage with the public on a regular basis, enjoy their work, making them dependable volunteers for any event.

In addition to sharing their stories and life experiences, retirees also have extensive social networks that can prove to be valuable tools for marketing and development activities. Many museums and galleries have auxiliary groups that help support their parent organization through special events and fundraising campaigns. A number of these groups are made up of retired professionals who recognize the value of your organization and have an interest in working to ensure the needs of the museum are met. Frequently, older volunteers learn about volunteer opportunities through their circle of friends and become active volunteers through repeated positive experiences at the museum.

As noted in the previous section, not all auxiliary groups fall under an institution's direct supervision, but many groups work closely with museum leadership to arrange events, help with activities, and partner in campaigns for the good of the organization. Maintaining positive relationships with the auxiliary group and its members secures a steady source of volunteers and volunteer advocates for many years.

Museums and galleries are prime places to provide learning opportunities. Retirees seek out opportunities to learn new skills or gain new knowledge in a field of their interest. Many of the volunteers in this group have worked in their profession for decades and are looking to expand their experiences into new

Seasoned volunteers have a wealth of knowledge to share with visitors and colleagues alike.

Image courtesy of the authors.

and different areas. In most cases, these volunteers also have a passion for lifelong learning and recognize the many benefits of engaging their minds in a variety of activities.

This drive to engage their mind in learning steers many of these volunteers to look for back-of-house volunteer opportunities like cataloging, database entry, and program development, as well as fundraising and publishing. One challenge with volunteers who are motivated to learn new skills is maintaining that drive to learn throughout a project. Some back-of-house projects can easily become stale or stagnant in the mind of the active learner, or complex projects can become overwhelming for a single volunteer learning new technology, languages, or skills. Retired volunteers may easily lose motivation to complete projects in which they are no longer engaged. Supervisors should provide learning opportunities on a regular basis to ensure the volunteer is engaged and continues to be committed to the museum and their projects.

Contrary to popular belief, the COVID-19 pandemic has not had a significant impact on retirement numbers. According to the United States Census Bureau's 2021 Survey of Income and Program Participation (SIPP), data collected shows only a modest number of pandemic-related retirements.[6] The percentage of individuals aged fifty-five to seventy who reported being retired actually saw a slight decline from January to December that year. When specifically asked about the pandemic's influence on their retirement plans, only 2.9 percent of adults in the same age group employed in January 2020 retired early or planned to retire early due to the pandemic. Similarly, 2.3 percent stated that they either delayed or planned to delay retirement for pandemic-related reasons. Therefore, it is evident that the retirement pool will continue to grow as anticipated, unaffected by the COVID-19 pandemic.

Looking ahead, the future of retired or post-career volunteers appears promising, as the number of retirees is set to increase in the coming years. With the last of the baby boom generation gradually completing their current careers and transitioning into retirement, this group will bring unique characteristics and needs to the volunteer landscape. Future retired volunteers will be more active than previous generations, driven by a growing emphasis on health and well-being in their daily lives. Studies have shown that participation in cultural activities prolongs health and well-being, and many organizations will develop programs and volunteer opportunities that will help their communities reach health and well-being goals.[7]

Additionally, studies have highlighted the positive impact of an active lifestyle on longevity. With a focus on health consciousness, the baby boomer generation and subsequent generations are expected to continue leading healthier lives, resulting in a larger pool of active volunteers. As community education continues to prioritize health, museums, and galleries can anticipate a bright future for retired volunteers in their institutions.

ENGAGING FAMILIES AND TEENS IN THE VOLUNTEER EXPERIENCE

A number of institutions, including children's museums, science museums, and historic homes, have embraced the opportunity to engage teenage and younger volunteers through a family volunteer program. Young volunteers are defined as children or students ages six to thirteen. Essentially, those who are too young to be considered a teen volunteer and are not yet legally able to work and volunteer for organizations on their own. While teenagers, usually those in high school (age sixteen) to early twenties, are able to seek out and volunteer in organizations on their own (but do check on your local labor laws regarding the youngest volunteers can work without parental supervision).

Children, teens, and family group volunteers can be beneficial to museums, especially when it comes to engaging other families with younger children, sharing stories about children from the past, and removing potential barriers for all visitors to help them experience the museum in a more whimsical way. When teens and families lead activities, visitors of all ages are more likely to get involved with the activity and maintain a stronger interest and engagement with the museum throughout their visit. Activities and positive engagement between visitors are the foundation of an extremely memorable experience. Repeat visitors become invested in the institution, ultimately leading to more involvement with the museum by becoming members or even active volunteers.

Family volunteers can be an organization's biggest advocate in the community, and families who volunteer together are key in strengthening bonds with the museum's community. As families volunteer, they get to know visitors and other volunteers, which in turn generates a close-knit community where museums can foster friendships and professional relationships through their volunteer programs and activities. The growth in teen volunteerism specifically can be attributed to the fact that many high schools require community volunteer hours as part of their curriculum and graduation requirements, and college admission officers view volunteer hours favorably.

Volunteer hours can push an applicant into the admit category for many colleges and universities worldwide. Community service ranks among the top five entrance criteria for colleges and universities by admission officers, according to the Community Service and College Admissions Survey.[8] Through the relationships built in service, teens can gain admittance to colleges and universities, or make connections to help them secure their first jobs, internships, or professional position after graduation.

A 2012 study conducted by DoSomething.org, which focused on teen volunteers and their importance for an organization and for their community, found that teens who are exposed to cultural organizations and volunteer opportunities early in their lives and working careers are more likely to maintain a sense of volunteerism throughout their teen years into adulthood and beyond.[9] Additionally, studies have shown that communities that have active

Families seek volunteer opportunities to engage in service of organizations that support family values.

Image courtesy of John Fino.

participants in cultural activities have lower rates of violence and school drop-outs, and volunteering from a young age builds more community empathy and a commitment to service well into adulthood. Museums that provide opportunities for local families will reap the benefit of building multigenerational relationships that will last well into the future.

The good news for you and your museum is that families and teens are interested in committing their time to engaging volunteer opportunities. It is your responsibility to ensure that opportunities are open and accessible to families and teens who express interest in your organization. While cultivating and managing opportunities for families and teens, there are a few important considerations to keep in mind. Because children and teens are legally considered minors, it is recommended that you have stricter criteria for accepting and managing family and teen volunteers. In addition to filling out the standard volunteer application, you have the option to specify certain age requirements or minimum qualifications. These qualifications may include at least one year of high school, additional on-site museum training, or certification in babysitting or first-aid, all of which can be required to be completed prior to volunteering without parental supervision.

For any volunteer, but especially students and teen volunteers, it is useful to request letters of reference. It is important that the volunteer acquires letters of reference from someone other than a relative, as this allows the volunteer manager the opportunity to learn about the volunteer's interests and experiences in a more professional manner. Teachers, employers, and guidance counselors make the best candidates to write letters for teen volunteers.

Like other volunteer groups, it is important to know how best to communicate with them. Young families and teens are online and living in the digital world more than any generation before them. While a phone call to a volunteer over the age of sixty-five to discuss a project is the best way to connect with them, families and students are more likely to prefer an email, text, or message through a social platform.

Like other volunteer groups, the social component of volunteering is important, and being able to connect with new friends and work on a project together motivates these volunteers above other groups. The DoSomething .org study found that 76 percent of teens who have friends who volunteer also volunteer, usually in the same organization. The study found that for "a young person, having friends that volunteer regularly is the primary factor influencing a young person's volunteering habits."[10]

Video conferencing programs, apps, and cloud-based software have made virtual communications and collaborative work easier for teams, and in some cases, volunteers may not even need to come into the organization to work on their projects. When working with younger volunteers, it is important to meet them on platforms where they already have a presence. Instead of relying solely on Teams or Zoom, consider using FaceTime or other social media apps that allow for communication. It is crucial to ensure that volunteers, of any age, understand and have access to the necessary tools for volunteering. For teens who are looking to fulfill their volunteer hours, or busy families interested in supporting an organization but cannot commit to on-site participation, the virtual option is a great way to connect with these volunteers.

The future of family and teen volunteering is bright. As long as there are engaging and exciting activities at local museums, families and teens will visit and volunteer for projects. Creating an effective communications plan will help keep these volunteers engaged and allow for opportunities to meet with peers, have play dates, and celebrate a job well done in a welcoming atmosphere—all key objectives to keeping this group coming back project after project or season after season to your museum.

INTERNS: GAINING CRUCIAL EXPERIENCE FOR THE FUTURE

Interns can be one of the most important volunteer groups for any organization as they bring dedication and professionalism to the museum and work closely with staff to learn the ins and outs of museum activities. Interns are generally college students or recent graduates who work for a definitive amount of time in order to gain specific professional skills, connections, and experience. Students are often encouraged to explore career paths through volunteerism and internships to find the right fit for their goals and aspirations. Lucky for museums and other nonprofits, the variety of skills needed to successfully run an organization can provide internships to nearly every type of degree-seeking student.

Before we explore the roles of interns in-depth, it is important to understand that while interns, specifically unpaid interns, are considered volunteers, internships do not fit the normal volunteer mold. Internships, if not properly supervised, can become unruly and unproductive. To ensure success for both the museum and intern, experiences must be entirely planned out in partnership with the college or university if course credit is involved, prior to the arrival of an intern. There are two main types of internships used in museums and galleries.

PAID INTERN

Any paid intern should be considered a paid, albeit temporary, employee of the institution. Their contracts typically last less than a year and reflect the dates their university or college may be in session. As temporary or contract employees, paid interns typically do not receive benefits like paid time off, pension contributions, or health insurance;[11] however, with the constant changes in employment law, this should be reviewed according to organization policies and employment law in your area.

If interns are classified as temporary employees, an organization will have to pay appropriate taxes, including social security, unemployment insurance, and workman's compensation in accordance with state laws. Alternatively, an institution can hire the intern on a contractual basis, in which case the contract employee may be responsible for paying such taxes on their own. The type of employment should be clearly defined and shared with the intern prior to their start date.

UNPAID INTERN

The unpaid intern is far more prevalent in nonprofits due to the many budget constraints museums and galleries face. Some communities and businesses believe interns should be paid when performing highly skilled work, especially when the organization offering the internship is financially stable. Many times, interns can be paid with funds from outside the organization, such as work-study, grants, or sponsorships. Since there is no official legislation regarding paid and unpaid internships, it is important to understand community expectations, and we would recommend making an effort to seek funding for your internship program, both to support the intern and their needs, as well as provide support for the person or department that will be supervising the intern.

A 2012 *Time* article titled "Hard Labor: Inside the Mounting Backlash against Unpaid Internships"[12] reported that one-third to one-half of all internships in the United States are unpaid. That number increases when you focus on solely nonprofit organizations such as museums or galleries. It is imperative for an organization to take special care of the intern program, as many former interns are suing their internship places under the Fair Labor Standards Act. The Fair Labor Standards Act was put in place in 1938, but in recent years it has been given a lot of attention as companies try to save money by sidestepping employment laws relating to internships and educational training. To determine whether an internship is eligible for volunteer (non-compensation) status, internship coordinators should use the Department of Labor's Test for Unpaid Interns.[13]

Interns' motivations are generally basic and usually related to their educational goals. They are college students or recent graduates who are looking for real-world experiences while using the skills and knowledge they acquired during their studies. Their motivation can be extremely personal; no two interns will seek the same experience in their volunteer roles. Some might be interested in breaking into a specific field while others seek to experience a new job or skill. Most interns see their end result as securing a paid position either at the organization where they are interning or at another, similar organization.

Since an intern's motivation and goals differ, it is very important to sit down with the intern and map out all of his or her motivations in order to develop realistic goals and outcomes for his or her internship. Museum internship coordinators must provide educational opportunities so that the intern's time can be spent developing skills, even if the project takes longer or uses more staff and museum resources as a result. Similar to teens and other student volunteers, any potential intern should submit an application packet. An intern application packet generally includes the following:

1. A one-page personal statement stating the intern's goals and how the museum can help them achieve those goals
2. A current resume or curriculum vitae
3. An institution application form
4. Letter(s) of reference from someone who is not directly involved in the internship application
5. Contact information of a professor or adviser overseeing the internship

In the fast-paced world of the twenty-first century, a growing number of post-secondary students are seeking out jobs that require an apprenticeship for specific skills rather than obtaining a four-year degree with many general studies requirements. However, this trend has not hindered the museum industry. Many trade schools and community colleges offer internship opportunities that can be applied in a museum setting. Students can complete internships in construction, restoration and preservation, landscaping, and architecture and design in historic houses, art galleries, national parks, and museums. The sky can be the limit when it comes to internship programs and opportunities. When developing a program, connect with local schools and training programs of all types to work out ways students can get involved with the organization.

REMOTE VOLUNTEERS: LEADING THE WAY IN VIRTUAL VOLUNTEERING

In the late twentieth century, the emergence of digital platforms presented museums with a unique opportunity to connect with a global audience. Websites, podcasts, social media, and other digital projects not only expanded the reach of these institutions but also paved the way for new visitor and volunteer demographics. Remote volunteering, also known as digital-based volunteering, has become increasingly crucial in recruiting and cultivating volunteers. This section explores the role of remote volunteers, their motivations, and why museums worldwide are embracing them as invaluable assets.

Prior to the COVID-19 pandemic, remote volunteering was already gaining traction in some museums as a means for volunteers to support institutions beyond their immediate community. It initially aimed to engage volunteers with nontraditional skill sets in the volunteer realm. However, the pandemic forced a technological shift upon those who were previously hesitant to embrace technology to explore ways they can stay connected with their community throughout the pandemic. The crisis compelled individuals to reevaluate how they could help and stay involved with their extended families, communities, and organizations like museums. It is hard to experience a crisis without seeing the renowned television personality Mr. Rogers and his words on memes on social media: *Look for the helpers.* As humans, we have an innate need to assist and help. The pandemic highlighted the significance of remote work, making digital-based volunteering more prominent than ever before.

Although the pandemic is considered over, the presence of remote volunteers is here to stay. You should work to develop specific programs and protocols tailored to remote volunteers. Slapping "REMOTE" on an old volunteer job description will not recruit or retain today's remote volunteer. You should ask yourself, *What can be done off-site?* Challenge yourself to look at your museum's needs with a different perspective of curiosity. Remote volunteer positions and on-site positions are not interchangeable. Some organizations prefer to train remote volunteers on site before transitioning to remote work, while other positions are entirely remote. Establishing a framework that accommodates remote volunteers is crucial for effective collaborations and engagement.

One critical aspect of any remote volunteer project is the technology required. In some instances, remote volunteers are expected to provide their own computers and devices for their assigned tasks. If this is the case, it should be noted on the volunteer listing and job description. Creating and managing expectations ensures that the partnership between the volunteer and you, the volunteer coordinator, begins with trust. It is essential to design projects that can be executed using basic programs accessible across different platforms. Requiring volunteers to purchase specialized software or hardware may discourage potential participants. To ensure a mutually beneficial experience, it is advisable to identify the interests, abilities, and needs of each volunteer, aligning them with suitable projects and the organization's objectives.

Regardless of the demographic or background of a volunteer, it is important to recognize that needs and activities change over time. An individual volunteer may fall into multiple categories discussed in this chapter. They may even move categories during their time at your organization. The world has seen serious change in the last ten years. Be open to shifting goals and expectations during the lifetime of a volunteer. It is important to acknowledge the diverse and multifaceted impact of COVID-19 on volunteerism.

While some volunteers have increased their efforts to support their communities during these challenging times, others have had to reduce their involvement due to shifting priorities and circumstances. Nevertheless, it is heartening to see that a significant portion of volunteers have remained dedicated, continuing to devote their time and energy to making a positive difference in their communities. You can foster lasting relationships with your volunteers by creating positive personal experiences for each individual.

When establishing a volunteer management program, it is crucial to take the time to observe and reflect on your organization's mission and its role in the community. By carefully analyzing your institution's needs and understanding

Providing remote volunteer opportunities opens the door to more volunteers for your organization.
Image in public domain.

the core group of volunteers, and potential volunteers, a solid foundation can be established for the volunteer program.

Not every volunteer will fall into these basic categories, and many will fall into more than one category. It is important that you and other leaders in your museum comprehend and understand the differences in each of their volunteer groups. Knowing what motivates a volunteer and how to keep them engaged with your organization will lead to mutually beneficial relationships for you, the volunteer, other museum staff, and the institution as a whole.

NOTES

1. American Alliance of Museums, Center for the Future of Museums (2021), Museums and Equity: Volunteers.
2. S. Jo, L. Paarlberg, and R. Nesbit, "Volunteering Behaviors of People of Color in the U.S. Communities: How Community Racial Composition Affects the Type of Organization People of Color Volunteer For," *Voluntas* 34 (2023): 760–76.
3. Hill Strategies, "Volunteers and Donors in Arts and Culture Organizations in Canada in 2013," 2016, https://hillstrategies.com/resource/volunteers-and-donors-in-arts -and-culture-organizations-in-canada-in-2013.
4. American Alliance of Museums, "Museum Facts," 2014, http://www.aam-us. org /about-museums/museum-facts.
5. Fidelity Charitable, "The Role of Volunteering in Philanthropy," 2020, https:// www.fidelitycharitable.org/content/dam/fc-public/docs/resources/the-role-of -volunteering-in-philanthropy.pdf.
6. Daniel Thompson, "Pandemic Disrupted Labor Markets but Had Modest Impact on Retirement Timing," https://www.census.gov (accessed September 19, 2022).
7. Helen Chatterjee, *Museums, Health and Well-Being* (London: Ashgate, 2013).
8. Miriam Salpeter, "Community Service Work Increasingly Important for College Applicants," *U.S. News Money*, November 30, 2011, http://money.usnews.com/money /blogs/outside-voices-careers/2011/11/30/communityservice-work-increasingly -important-for-college-applicants.
9. DoSomething.org, "The DoSomething.org Index on Young People and Volunteering: The Year of Friends with Benefits," https://dosomething-a.akamaihd.net/sites /default/files/blog/2012-Web-Singleview_0.pdf.
10. DoSomething.org, "The DoSomething.org Index."
11. United States Department of Labor, "Fact Sheet #71: Internship Programs under the Fair Labor Standards Act," April 2010, http://www.dol.gov/whd/regs/compliance /whdfs71.htm.
12. Josh Sanburn, "Hard Labor: Inside the Mounting Backlash against Unpaid Internships," *Time*, May 21, 2012, https://content.time.com/time/subscriber/article/0 ,33009,2114428,00.html.
13. United States Department of Labor, "Fact Sheet #71."

3

Making a List and Checking It Twice

PLANNING A VOLUNTEER PROGRAM

By identifying a need for volunteer support at your organization and understanding the unique dynamics of your community, you have already taken the first steps toward creating a successful volunteer program. You have connected with internal and external partners, gathering valuable insights and perspectives that will move the organization forward, and you have identified ways to make those opportunities accessible and reflective of your community. Now it is time to dive into the nitty-gritty details and begin to build or finesse your volunteer program. From outlining tasks and procedures to creating necessary forms, this chapter will guide you through a step-by-step process to support you in creating a successful and impactful volunteer program at your museum.

When a volunteer steps in the door to start their first shift, it is the culmination of months of work between curators, educators, department heads, and volunteer coordinators. As needs are identified by museum staff members, the hope is they will contact you, the volunteer coordinator, to get the ball rolling on creating a worthwhile project for the institution and the volunteer. Although we recommend that one person at the organization be the point person for managing volunteers and their projects, we know that it is not always feasible. Luckily, there are tools to help keep the leadership team at any museum organized (such as Google apps, project management software, and even some CRMs). We encourage all organizations to identify what organizational solution works best for the team and budget. As your program grows, more robust solutions may be an option.

Regardless of what tools you use, cloud-based software for communication, scheduling, and project management will be an invaluable tool for your team. To get started, upload any current and relevant documents into a folder that is accessible by those who manage volunteers. This could include orientation booklets, timesheets, applications, project outlines, contact lists, and other valuable volunteer knowledge. We like to organize our documents in subfolders, but do what works best for your organization. Be sure to grant access to those who need the tools for effective volunteer management.

CREATING A VOLUNTEER HANDBOOK FOR THE ORGANIZATION

The first step for any solid volunteer program is to create a handbook for volunteer management. Much like this book, your handbook will provide some basic historical information about your organization, contacts for volunteers and their managers, special dates and events that should be on the volunteer annual calendar, and general policies and procedures for the organization. You may likely want two handbooks, one for the volunteer to take with them (like an orientation book or guide) and one for the organization to have as a reference for managing volunteers and projects (like a human resources reference file). We will break both of these handbooks down for you further in this section.

When you are just starting out, this can feel overwhelming to tackle, but grab a nice cup of coffee or a snack and just brain dump all the information you know and want to share with your volunteers. You will find your pages fill up quickly! Afterward, you can go back and organize important information for the handbook. These are living, dynamic documents, which means that you can edit them as your volunteer program evolves. Just make sure to share changes with your leadership and your volunteers to keep everyone on the same page and working toward common goals.

If you still feel overwhelmed, take out your staff handbook and thumb through it for inspiration. What important information can be shared with your volunteers in order to help them familiarize and orient themselves to the culture and expectations of the organization? You will want to be sure to include any staff policies or procedures such as dress codes. It may be necessary for volunteers working at a historic site to wear period costumes or use personal protective equipment, such as steel-toed shoes when working in the collections area.

Other details to communicate include instructions on parking and accessing buildings, as well as the specific shift timings and your site's opening hours. Include contact information for the front desk, volunteer and project coordinators, emergency contacts on site, and maybe even local emergency services.

Like staff, your volunteers may find it very useful and empowering to have a copy of the mission, vision, and an outline of strategic priorities. This not only helps them communicate important information about the organization to visitors, but it also helps volunteers recognize and understand their value within the organization. Creating a volunteer department mission statement is another great item to include to help volunteers stay motivated and engaged with their projects and the museum at large.

Many museums rely on volunteers to help with special events throughout the year. Annual events become staples in the community and volunteers and visitors alike enjoy reconnecting at these events. By including a calendar and identifying the potential volunteer requirements for each event, volunteers will be able to proactively plan for upcoming opportunities that align with their interests. This allows them to reserve the necessary time slots in their personal calendars so that they are well-prepared to contribute.

Last, many volunteers are drawn to museum volunteering to continue their educational journey, learn new skills, or research interesting topics. Consider providing tips, tricks, or tools-of-the-trade bulletins as part of your donor communications. It could be something they add to their physical or digital personal binders while working with you. If you have access to online resources, consider sharing login information so that volunteers can check out resources at times that are convenient for them.

Overall, a volunteer handbook or orientation binder should include all the information a volunteer may need to stay on track with their project while supporting the mission of the museum to its fullest. Take a moment to think about what you would appreciate knowing when starting your volunteer journey. Perhaps you can include the most common questions from your current volunteers in your new orientation binder. This book will help you create your volunteer job description templates and help guide the interview process as well, if you have sorted your needs and expectations out prior to engaging with new volunteers.

From our experience, we can confirm that volunteers certainly appreciate the time that goes into preparing a welcome package for them. They are empowered when they have the tools to find the answers they need for themselves. Do not be afraid to include "too much" information, as it will likely be just the right amount for a volunteer as they grow in their time with you.

Volunteers can contribute to on-site and off-site programs as well as special events.
Image courtesy of the authors.

IDENTIFYING NEED FOR VOLUNTEER HELP

Creating a successful volunteer program or project requires careful planning and organization. While it may seem tedious, the initial steps of identifying needs, filling out forms, and fielding internal requests are vital in establishing a strong foundation for your volunteer program. You should rely on these activities, procedures, and policies to efficiently recruit, manage, and build your volunteer corps. It is crucial to consider how each need of the museum can be fulfilled by volunteers with varying abilities. This exploration allows museums to make sure that their community is well represented and that all individuals have the opportunity to contribute their unique skills and perspectives. By recognizing the importance of these initial steps and considering the diverse abilities of potential volunteers, you can create a robust and inclusive program that benefits your institution and the community it serves.

By creating inclusive volunteer opportunities, you are making certain that everyone in the community feels welcome and valued. A strategic approach to achieving this goal is to actively involve local representatives from diverse backgrounds in the planning and execution of your volunteer opportunities. By inviting them to the table, you will be able to tap into their perspectives and insights, enabling you to identify specific needs and design volunteer opportunities that welcome volunteers with a range of abilities and knowledge.

Additionally, establishing a community advisory board can provide a platform for community members to share their experiences and suggestions, helping to shape the program in a truly collaborative way. Speaking of collaboration, when focusing on diversity, equity, inclusion, and accessibility (DEIA) opportunities, do not reinvent the wheel. That is to say that your community may already have established organizations like work readiness programs, local The Arc[1] chapters (an organization supporting inclusionary opportunities for a range of developmental abilities), and organizations that promote inclusivity and empowerment. Partnering with these groups can provide valuable resources and a direct line to a whole new volunteer pool.

No matter how small or large your volunteer management team is (whether it consists of only one person or an entire office), when a need for a volunteer is identified, it is considered best practice to have any requests documented in writing. We have all been in situations where impromptu meetings happen in hallways or last-minute requests arise at the end of a long meeting. It typically starts with a casual "by the way"; and as any volunteer coordinator can attest, it often leads to a request for volunteers.

While networking with your colleagues is invaluable, having a protocol for internal volunteer asks can save you a lot of trouble and stress in the long run. When you establish a process for addressing internal volunteer needs, you can simply direct your coworkers to a volunteer request form, making the whole process more organized and efficient.

Committees are a great way to get more volunteers involved in museum operations.
Image courtesy of The National EMS Museum.

Conversely, you and other museum staff may get requests from external professionals, students, or community members looking for volunteer opportunities. It is important to evaluate external requests in order to make sure the request aligns with internal needs and opportunities. By doing so, you will be able to guarantee that you have the necessary resources available and that any proposed project contributes to your museum's mission. Any request for volunteers should include the department requesting the volunteer, a contact name and information, a brief description of the project, a priority level, and a timeline for the project. This information will be necessary when it comes time to create the volunteer job description and announcement for the position.

JOB DESCRIPTIONS AND RECRUITING

Job descriptions for volunteer opportunities are the foundation of volunteer recruitment. To potential volunteers, they provide a clear understanding of the responsibilities and expectations associated with the role. For seasoned volunteers, they serve as a reference point, providing them with a clear understanding of their duties. They establish a structured framework for the proper handling of responsibilities by volunteers, while also setting objective criteria for them to meet. By outlining the rules to follow, job descriptions lay the foundation for continued success in their roles. Without a job description, potential

Internal Volunteer Request Form

If you would like to request a volunteer for a project, please fill out the form and return it to the volunteer manager.

Name_____Department_____

Date Requested _____ Date Needed_____

Is this project ongoing?_____ If no, date it will be completed_____

Briefly describe the project

_____

_____

_____

_____

_____

What hard skills are required?

_____

_____

What soft skills are required?

_____

_____

What is the priority of the request? (critical, important, nice to have)

_____

Project approval

Manager sign off_____

Deputy Director sign off_____

Sample Internal Volunteer Request From.
Image courtsey of the authors.

volunteers may not fully grasp what they are signing up for, which can lead to misunderstandings and dissatisfaction down the line.

Having clear job descriptions helps set expectations for volunteers and empowers them to meet and exceed those expectations. When your volunteers understand their responsibilities, they are more likely to feel fulfilled and motivated in their roles. On the other hand, not meeting a volunteer's expectations can lead to frustration and dissatisfaction, potentially causing them to disengage from the project or worse, leave your organization.

The volunteer job description should include information on the project or duties the volunteer will work on, any required skills or qualifications, any necessary accommodations, the minimum time commitment expected, the department the volunteer will be supporting, and any general information about being a volunteer in your organization. When creating job descriptions, utilize the completed volunteer request form for details. This ensures that all relevant details are included in the job description and that nothing is overlooked. By involving the department or project supervisors directly, volunteer managers can accurately capture the requirements and expectations of the role.Sample Volunteer Job Description.

Like any paid position, job postings are an important way to communicate an organization's need for help. A volunteer job posting should be attention-grabbing and effectively communicate the key details of the position. It should not only outline the expectations and responsibilities of the role but also provide a brief overview of the qualifications desired in an ideal candidate. The posting should include clear contact information and application instructions for interested individuals.

It is important to consider the design of any application and announcements. Make the posting inviting, colorful, and energetic. If you are using a graphic, make it active (people working and having a good time) or use emoji and graphic artwork to hint at what the opportunity has in store. Remember to embed accessible language or post with a description (not just a JPEG image) when making an announcement on any digital platform. Many potential volunteers rely on digital assistance to get their news, emails, and social feeds. You have prepared yourself and the organization for volunteers; now you want to excite the right people to join your team!

When seeking volunteers, museums can effectively advertise their needs through various channels. In addition to traditional methods like posting on their websites or reaching out to local volunteer organizations, museums have found success in leveraging social media platforms. They can join relevant social media groups and engage with local communities through platforms like Facebook, Reddit, and Nextdoor.

Museums also utilize professional networking and job search sites like LinkedIn and Indeed.com as avenues of recruitment. Once only reserved for paid positions, these sites now promote a wider range of opportunities, including unpaid opportunities. Utilizing popular hashtags such as #Volunteer or #MuseumVolunteer can also attract potential volunteers. Word-of-mouth is another valuable strategy, where current volunteers, staff, and board members can personally communicate the museum's needs to their friends and social circles.

When you promote volunteer opportunities through social channels, it is essential to provide basic information about the job, the organization, the tasks involved, the time commitment, and the appropriate contact person for

Volunteer Job Description
Education Department

Position: Exhibit Interpreter or House Volunteer

Supervisor: Education Manager, Volunteer Coordinator
                 Other Managers as appropriate

Objective: To assist with the interpretation of the historic house and to
                 educate the public regarding the collections and exhibits.

Responsibilities:
- Greet guests to the historic house
- Provide general and specific information about the residence and its occupants
- Interpret the history of the house
- Encourage inquiry and dialog
- Report any maintenance issues
- Enforce safety rules and assist with guest safety

Qualifications:
- Enthusiasm for history; Knowledge of museum and related topics.
- Enthusiasm for speaking with visitors; good communication skills.
- Ability to assist with some or all of the tasks listed above.

Training: Training in general site interpretation. Training and direction for individual
                 projects will be provided.

Requirements: Set a specific day of the week and time you will volunteer.

expressing interest. These social job announcements tend to be less detailed, as they are targeted at audiences already familiar with the museum's mission and ongoing projects, who understand the role without the need for a formal position description.

Other museums have found success in going to volunteer and job fairs or visiting local senior centers, businesses, universities, and high schools to discuss volunteer opportunities with potential volunteers directly. These events are considered outreach, and you may find that you are not the only one in your museum that attends outreach events. Volunteer recruitment can indeed be everyone's job, and involving your colleagues in the process can help widen the reach and make a bigger impact. By educating your colleagues and other volunteers about new volunteer opportunities and the application process, they can also speak to the volunteer needs at your organization when they are out in the community.

Creating a volunteer information packet for others in your museum is a great idea to support this effort. Including volunteer flyers, business cards for collecting more information, and job descriptions for actively recruited positions can provide coworkers with all the necessary details that can be passed on to potential volunteers. This can be a physical packet of paper or a digital packet on your website and can be distributed at outreach events via QR code or even kept readily available at your museum.

Regardless of who is doing the outreach, the number of touches (or people with whom you made contact) should be taken into account when evaluating the success of each outreach activity. These statistics can help you understand the effectiveness of your recruitment efforts and guide future participation in recruitment activities and events. Additionally, keeping track of numbers can also measure how equitable the events are, as you can assess the diversity and inclusivity of the individuals you are engaging with. Remember, by involving everyone in volunteer recruitment and being mindful of outreach efforts, you can create a collaborative and inclusive environment that attracts a diverse group of volunteers to support your museum's mission.

Prior to going to an off-site recruitment event, certain preparations should be made. You should have identified needs or positions that will be filled by volunteers and have supervisors prepared to take on new volunteers after the event and subsequent application process. On the day of the event, you should bring job descriptions for open positions, business cards or museum contact information, and volunteer applications with you. A sign-up sheet for those who would like more information but are not ready to commit should also be provided.

Recruitment fairs are highly competitive events, and there are usually a number of other nonprofits ranging from national charities to local shelters, welfare groups, and clubs vying for volunteers. A successful recruitment booth has audio/visual props such as pictures, videos, music, or a combination of media that illustrate not only the jobs that volunteers can sign up for but also rewards offered to volunteers, such as lectures, events, parties, and gifts that volunteers receive as thanks for their commitment. If possible, you can recruit volunteers to come with you to these events. They can speak about their experiences and encourage any potential volunteer by giving firsthand accounts and examples of what it is like volunteering at the museum or gallery.

Some museums have even conducted recruiting events at their museum. By hosting an open house and inviting the public to visit the museum and meet curators, educators, and other staff, potential volunteers can learn about ways they can get involved with the institution. These types of events may require more staff time for preparation, but they can be very successful in connecting with people directly and allowing volunteers to meet museum staff that will

Sharing areas of need helps potential volunteers think of ways they can contribute to the museum.
Image courtesy of the authors.

help them with their application process before committing to a volunteer position.

Successful volunteer recruitment does not have to be limited to certain events or outreach campaigns. Recruitment should be happening all of the time, especially in small museums, which may not have sufficient staff to attend off-site recruitment events. Front desk or admission staff, store associates, and frontline gallery staff should also have access to the volunteer information packet so that they can provide visitors who are interested in volunteering with accurate and appropriate information. Frontline staff should likewise be trained to recognize various levels of interest in guests and provide the necessary contact information for the volunteer coordinator.

You may not have time to meet with everyone who shows interest in volunteering throughout the day. When able, an effort should be made to take a few minutes to meet with any potential volunteer. In this brief time, you can answer any questions they may have, or you can set up a time to formally meet and discuss volunteer opportunities. If you are not available, empower front-of-house staff to give the potential volunteer your business card or even a volunteer application. They could even go as far as collecting pertinent information for you, then you can follow up with more details.

In addition to staff members recruiting, some museums have information about their volunteer program in their lobby. Advertising on site and in the galleries has several benefits. In-gallery advertisements can grab potential volunteers while they are inspired by the organization and its collections. Having a link to a digital application or requesting a call back from the volunteer coordinator helps get the ball rolling at the moment.

As with other commitments, once a volunteer leaves the museum, they are going to get busy with life and may forget to submit an application without any prompting. Partner with your development and marketing team to create engaging posters or flyers that not only promote volunteer opportunities but also highlight various other ways a visitor can contribute to your museum. When a museum posts signage for both volunteer opportunities and membership information, the visitor is reminded that the museum is a nonprofit organization, and it relies on the goodwill of visitors and community members. This type of advertisement encourages engagement through either volunteerism or philanthropy, both of which help promote the mission of the organization to the community at large.

To effectively recruit volunteers, it is important to share volunteer opportunities in various places. This can include the organization's website and social media channels, community bulletin boards, schools, personal networks, and even the board network if applicable. By sharing opportunities in multiple locations, you can reach a wider audience and attract individuals who may be interested in contributing their time and skills.

Job descriptions play a vital role in volunteer recruitment. They provide clarity and set expectations for potential volunteers, ensuring that they have a clear understanding of the role they are taking on. By meeting and exceeding these expectations, organizations can enhance volunteer recruitment and retention rates. Sharing volunteer opportunities through various channels also helps attract a diverse pool of volunteers who can contribute their talents to the organization's mission.

APPLICATION AND INTERVIEWING

Written job descriptions, requests for volunteers, and job announcements help the volunteer manager clearly outline the role and expectations for a potential volunteer. Applications, and subsequent volunteer interviews, are important steps to ensure a successful volunteer program not only to introduce opportunities to potential volunteers and potential volunteers to the museum but also to align expectations, goals, and rewards for volunteers and the museum.

In many instances, when a volunteer experiences failure, discouragement, or dissatisfaction in their role, it can be attributed to a mismatch between their expectations and the reality of the job or project. Job descriptions are there for both the volunteer and the project manager to mitigate miscommunication and align goals. The volunteer job description should be included in any volunteer

Sample Volunteer Information Flyer.
Image courtesy of the authors.

listings. Copies should also be made available to volunteers, either in paper or electronic form.

When crafting a job description, collaboration between the project manager and volunteer manager is paramount to ensure that the position aligns with the skills and interests of potential volunteers. If necessary, tasks can be divided into smaller parts or distributed among a team of volunteers rather than being assigned to a single individual. The job description should clearly state the position title, necessary qualifications or experiences, project objectives, and the type of activity the volunteer should expect to perform on a regular basis.

Like employment applications, volunteer applications ask for basic information. An application typically requires the following items:

1. *Name*: The applicant's full name is necessary for identification purposes.
2. *Address*: The applicant's current residential address is needed for communication and contact information.
3. *Zip code*: The zip code helps in determining regional location and demographics.
4. *Birthday*: The applicant's date of birth is required for age verification and legal purposes.
5. *Place of employment or former place of employment*: Providing information about their current or past employers helps assess their work history and experience.
6. *References*: Including references allows the employer to contact individuals who can vouch for the applicant's skills, character, and work ethic.
7. *Interests*: Sharing personal interests helps the employer understand the applicant's hobbies and potential cultural fit within the organization.
8. *How they found the opportunity*: Knowing how the applicant discovered the job opening or opportunity helps the employer evaluate their recruitment efforts and sources.

These details on an application form enable employers to assess an applicant's background, qualifications, and suitability for the position.Sample Volunteer Application.

Image courtesy of the authors.

During the application process, it may be appropriate to ask a volunteer to include a résumé or curriculum vitae for additional information when applying for a specific volunteer position, especially if the position requires professional experience. You can then use these applications to get to know a little about the potential volunteer and create interview talking points, similar to a professional job interview. Applications should be one to two pages at the most, as many volunteers could be discouraged by a lengthy application process and may look for opportunities at organizations that are easier to get into. Applications are a way to collect basic information to assess the potential volunteer for an interview and eventual placement in the organization.

Once an application is received, you as well as the potential volunteer's supervisor should review it. Once an applicant meets the project requirements, it is time to schedule a meeting or interview to further explore their interest and

Art Museum Adult Volunteer Application

First Name: _____ Last Name:_____

Preferred Name: _____ Pronouns:_____

Address:_____

City:_____ State: _____

Zip:_____County: _____ Phone #: _____

Email: _____

Do you consent to a criminal background check? ☐Yes ☐ No

About You

Are you a Museum Member? ☐Yes ☐ No

Do other members of your family volunteer or work the Art Museum? ☐ Yes ☐ No

If yes, please list their names below:

_____

How did you hear about the Volunteer Program?

_____

_____

Why do you want to volunteer at the Art Museum?

_____

Do you hold any certifications or licensures? ☐ Yes ☐ No

If yes, please list: _____ _____

List any hobbies, skills, talents, or training that you would like us to know about:_____

Are you a volunteer for any other organization? ☐Yes ☐ No

List volunteer positions of interest _____

discuss the project in greater detail. Once an application is accepted and the volunteer moves on to an interview, a volunteer personnel file should be created to hold all the important documentation related to the volunteer's work. Applications, along with job descriptions, are generally the first items in a volunteer's folder and can be referenced during their time at the organization.

Instead of relying on traditional paper files, a more efficient and convenient approach is to keep volunteer files digitally. You can achieve this through the use of various technologies and software applications. By scanning physical documents and converting them into digital files, you can store and organize their personal information electronically. You can even skip the physical paperwork and create digital forms and other necessary documentation to be shared via email or through team folders.

No matter your solution at this step of the process, remember to consider those volunteers who may use assistance devices or technology and be prepared to accommodate their needs appropriately through technology or paper documentation. Cloud storage services, such as Google Drive or Dropbox, provide secure platforms for storing and accessing these digital files from anywhere, at any time. Additionally, password-protected folders and encryption methods ensure the confidentiality and privacy of sensitive information. Digitizing personnel files not only saves physical space but also simplifies the process of searching, editing, and sharing documents, making it a more streamlined and environmentally friendly option.An interview questionnaire helps keep a volunteer interview on track.

The interview phase may be the first opportunity for potential volunteers to form their first impression of your program and museum. The interview will set the tone and expectations for the volunteer throughout their time with you and your organization. Just like interviewing an employment candidate, it is important that you cover all the basic information a volunteer needs to know about their role, generally, in the interview—from time commitments, schedules, and job responsibilities to special training and skills needed for the position, as well as addressing questions and concerns that the potential volunteer has about the role.

It is in both of your best interests to outline clear expectations and responsibilities when interviewing a new volunteer. To help ensure that volunteers have all the information they need, some volunteer managers create a checklist of questions that they ask all volunteers, and they make notes regarding a specific volunteer's interests and skills on the questionnaire. The questionnaire can also be shared with the volunteer's supervisor if they are not able to attend an interview and make their notes about the volunteer.

If a formal interview questionnaire is filled out during the interview, then that form should also be included in the volunteer's file for reference in the event of questions or conflict arising from the position. The questionnaire can

Volunteer Interview Questionnaire

Volunteer name:_____   Staff Interviewer:_____

What interested you about this volunteer position?

Tell me the story of how your chose your education program/ career path / life work?

Have you volunteered in the past? What have you enjoyed most about previous volunteer work?

Are you involved in other organized activities?

What would be the ideal volunteer job for you – and why?

Can you briefly talk about your experiences as they relate to this position?

What would you say are three of your strengths?

What are your expectations of our organization? Of our employees?

What are your personal goals for this experience?

Do you have any questions that you would like to ask us?

also be referenced if the volunteer requests another job assignment instead of another formal interview.

ONBOARDING AND MENTORSHIP: BUILDING A SUCCESS TEAM

Congratulations, you have worked with colleagues to create opportunities for volunteers to engage in your mission, you have worked on building up your foundational documents, posted the opportunity all over town, and you have interviewed potential volunteers. You have your team ready to go, but let's make sure they get started on the right foot.

Using the onboarding manual you already created, it is vital to have any new volunteer participate in a face-to-face or virtual onboarding session. This session can introduce them to their new teammates and allows you to reinforce the museum's mission, project goals, and objectives with the team. Establishing a solid groundwork for the team fosters a sense of unity and ensures that everyone starts with the necessary knowledge and resources to be successful. This helps individuals feel that they are all on the same page, and it sets the stage for a productive and cohesive team dynamic. Whether you are onboarding board members, team leaders, or any one of your amazing volunteers, you will want to make time to allow for exploration and reflection on the part of your volunteers.

Be respectful of their time and try to coordinate onboarding sessions as part of their normal shift schedule. You can also have a few alternative times outside of the typical business hours for meetings or training sessions. If you are doing an in-person meeting, consider putting together an agenda to help everyone know what goals you have for the day and to help keep the group on track. Allow time for questions and conversation but be sure to maintain your agenda to ensure that all the important items are covered in your time together. And if you are able, we suggest providing a few treats or refreshments as a hungry or thirsty volunteer is hard to keep focused.

If you are doing your onboarding sessions via online platforms, consider your timeframe and technology. Attention spans are not what they used to be, and it is best to keep sessions under an hour. Make sure all the material you want to share with your volunteers is accessible before your session so that a volunteer can print the material, translate it, or upload it to accessible devices as needed. Ensure that your Wi-Fi network is as strong as possible (or you are hardwired into your provider) and that you can navigate some basic troubleshooting for your volunteers if the need arises.

Like the rest of your volunteer program, with a little bit of planning and open lines of communication, your onboarding experience will be amazingly encouraging and set your volunteers up for success over the long term.

LEADING A CHAMPIONSHIP TEAM

Building a strong and sustainable volunteer base requires a plan for ongoing support and training for your volunteers. From mentorship to structured training, to informal learning opportunities, investing in training opportunities for your volunteers to acquire the necessary knowledge and skills to effectively contribute to the organization should remain a priority throughout your program.

Many organizations have created opportunities for staff, experienced volunteers, or advisory groups to serve as team leaders. You may want to have lead volunteers who take on more responsibility and leadership roles. In many cases having a lead volunteer can be beneficial as they can support your work by being more hands-on with the team. They may be more familiar with the needs of other volunteers on the team and what challenges may be arising with their projects. Lead volunteers can be eyes on the ground and provide an extra helping hand in making sure volunteers are settling into their roles, feeling positive about their work, identifying challenges with their team, and advocating for needs as they arise.

Having lead volunteers and volunteer teams can introduce new challenges to you as the volunteer coordinator. You have to put your trust in your lead volunteers to work with compassion and have impeccable communication with their team members. Volunteers who work on teams may not feel as connected to the staff they work alongside as they are not directly checking in with staff and coordinating their projects together.

It is worthwhile to make an extra effort to check in and be present with as much as you can when volunteers are on site as well as participate in meetings just to show your support and be able to answer questions. It is also important to check on your lead volunteers regularly to ensure they are comfortable with their role and are not feeling unnecessary pressure or are at risk of burnout in their role. The last thing you want is for a volunteer to feel worn out, frustrated, or discouraged but feel obligated to continue because they are responsible for the team's success.

Establishing teams with a lead volunteer is a great way to make a bigger impact on your organization through the volunteer program; while there may be some challenges, such as increased expectations and potential burnout, having invested individuals who are dedicated to the cause and can motivate others with their passion can greatly enhance the long-term success of the volunteer program.

Another important component in creating a champion volunteer team is to help your fellow staff members understand the role of volunteers. Often, whether unintentionally or not, staff can become overburdened with their work and see some tasks as "so simple" that a volunteer can do the work without training or supervision. Have you heard a colleague say, "It's just a quick project stuffing envelopes" or "I just need someone to wipe down these desks or toys?" Although these tasks are quick and simple to do, they are not the ideal jobs for a volunteer because they are quick, less meaningful jobs that nonprofits in general should have their staff handle.

On the other hand, volunteers should have more rewarding tasks that reflect their values and commitment to the organization. This is not to say that some volunteers might offer to help as part of event clean-up or on a day when they just want to come to socialize with friends and do a small task at the same time, but those are special days and part of a bigger plan for the volunteer.

As a volunteer coordinator, it is your responsibility to educate staff, and maybe even your volunteer leaders and board members about your volunteer program and what your mission and motivations are in recruiting and supporting volunteers. You can highlight your current volunteers, their motivations, and their capacity to serve through monthly spotlights for the organization (think of those internal newsletters and updates we get, can you add a Volunteer Spotlight or Rising Volunteer Star to those communications).

Help staff understand that they need to coordinate work with you and your department, even if it is a small task like setting up tables and chairs for an event. Keeping lines of communication open helps build your relationship with colleagues, and you will learn to anticipate their needs as the year progresses, making volunteer coordination easier for everyone.

It is also your job to maintain the distinction between paid staff and volunteers and ensure that necessary accommodations for any work area are met to the standards your volunteers require. It is not uncommon for colleagues to assume that certain tasks can simply be handed off to a volunteer without considering the accessibility and training needs or the complexity and value of the volunteer's contributions to the organization. Therefore, it is crucial that you provide training and resources to educate staff on how to effectively interact with, support, and appreciate volunteers.

Sharing articles about volunteer management with other departments can help foster a culture of understanding and appreciation throughout the organization. You can also create and distribute a Volunteer 101 help sheet for your museum. A Volunteer 101 help sheet is a valuable tool that you can create to provide resources to the leadership and employees of your museum. It is essential because other colleagues may have little to no experience supervising and working with volunteers. Some may feel uncertain about how to effectively plan and collaborate with them. There might be misconceptions that volunteers cannot face consequences for their actions or that staff members lack the authority to correct or motivate volunteers on a daily basis.

By including key information such as the motivations of volunteers, strategies to maintain volunteer satisfaction, ways to celebrate volunteers, and clear definitions of the roles and responsibilities of volunteers, creating this help sheet will empower and serve as a collective resource that encourages collaboration among the staff, fostering a positive and productive environment for volunteers and employees alike. Remember, these items can also go into a volunteer management binder for staff, as mentioned in section one of this chapter. While you play the primary role in recruitment and retention, it is the collective responsibility of the entire organization to ensure the long-term engagement and satisfaction of volunteers.

In this chapter, we have looked at all the materials that go into creating a champion volunteer program at any organization. These components range from collaborating with colleagues to identify the need for volunteers, creating a comprehensive plan and job descriptions, and effectively recruiting and managing your team. Each of these steps contributes to building a solid foundation for a robust and successful volunteer team right from the start. We encourage you to reference this chapter as each new opportunity for volunteer engagement is identified.

While certain projects may not require such detailed management, it is still beneficial to go through the exercises for each opportunity. This ensures that all staff and volunteers have a clear understanding of their expectations and outcomes, while also guaranteeing that accessibility needs are addressed and met, and that volunteers feel valued and included in the project. It will also leave you, your team leaders, and any supervising staff the tools to feel confident in supervising the task at hand, effectively communicating the volunteer needs and achievements, and tackling any challenges that may arise throughout the project.

In the next chapter, we will look more closely at strategies to manage and foster long-term success within your volunteer corps making all the work you have accomplished through this chapter a winning formula for success!

NOTE

1. The Arc Website, https://www.thearc.org (accessed August 31, 2023).

4

Plotting the Course

THE LIFE CYCLE OF A VOLUNTEER

Managing a team of volunteers is a large job at any organization. From project development and recruiting to training, troubleshooting, and celebrating accomplishments, volunteer coordinators are responsible for ensuring the safety and well-being of volunteers throughout their institution day in and day out. In order to successfully manage volunteers, coordinators and supervisors need to effectively communicate with a variety of people and across a multitude of media when relaying important information, such as schedule changes and institutional news, to their volunteers.

The previous chapter explored what tasks are necessary to attract new volunteers and get them in the door. But what do you do with them once you have decided they are the right fit for the organization and the project? In this chapter, we will explore ways to support your volunteer team so they can be successful in their roles and contribute meaningfully to your organization while also exploring strategies and tools that can help make your job of coordinating volunteers easier. Please refer to the previous chapter and this chapter often to ensure that your foundation is solid and your program is growing in a supportive and robust way.

Like other departments in a museum, volunteer departments need to be reflective of changes that take place in the organization and the community around the museum. Being engaged in active dialog with museum leadership, staff, volunteers, visitors, and the community at large will help to make certain your volunteer program and opportunities are inclusive and reflective of your mission and goals, and of course welcomed and supported by your visitors, donors, and neighbors.

GETTING STARTED

On day one, your priority is to create a smooth onboarding process that sets the right expectations and ensures the volunteer is set up for success. An onboarding plan should include a welcome meeting for the volunteer, a tour of the site and workspace or digital platforms, and an introduction to colleagues around the organization. The welcome meeting is just the beginning of orientation and should introduce volunteers to the organization and its mission. To help capture the culture and provide support and guidance, you could institute an onboarding buddy program by pairing more seasoned volunteers with new volunteers. This offers the new volunteer a friendly and experienced point of contact as they move through orientation. This is also the time to secure training dates and future schedules. These steps create a seamless transition between the interview stage and actively volunteering.

During this period, a tour of the site, the volunteer's workspace, and the digital platforms they will be using will help the new volunteers orient themselves to the activities they will be performing at the museum. We have found it helpful to start with a general tour of the site, much like a visitor would take, and then take the new volunteer on a behind-the-scenes tour ensuring they know where to find the break rooms, restrooms, supply areas, and other spaces that will help them adjust quickly to their surroundings.

If you are onboarding a virtual volunteer, a tour of the virtual experience is just as important as an on-site tour of the museum. Many virtual volunteers have a level of comfort with technology, but each platform can behave in different ways. Use this opportunity to show these quirks to volunteers so they can successfully navigate a technological challenge on their own. During this time, you can also help them differentiate between a simple quirk and when they should contact you, their project manager, or the system administrator to help with troubleshooting.

Regular opportunities to connect with volunteers is a great way to build a healthy volunteer team.
Image courtesy of Wikimedia.

These experiences also give you, the volunteer coordinator, dedicated time to casually meet with your new volunteer and learn a bit more about them. Take time to learn how they best communicate and work, where they are most comfortable in their skills, and where some additional training might be useful, or if there are ways to adjust the project to make the job easier, safer, and more enjoyable for the volunteer. This is your time to learn as much as you can about how you can support them in their volunteer journey.

Throughout your welcome meeting, tours, and other activities with a new volunteer, be sure to introduce them to colleagues as you encounter them. Many volunteers are excited to get to work, but then find they do not know who to go to for help, or even who to say hi to when walking in the building for their first solo shift. It helps put everyone at ease when there are known friendly faces around the museum to help with questions, directions, or just a quick chat during a coffee break. Take the time to help establish connections for your new volunteers, and use the opportunity to connect with more-established volunteers as well. A quick complement of work during an introduction makes a lasting impression on many volunteers, especially if they do not get to work with you or other staff regularly. Having a volunteer corps who enjoy connecting with each other regularly helps build a strong and successful team to help carry the mission of the museum forward day in and day out.

To prevent losing volunteers in the time between interviews and training, you should confirm training dates shortly after a volunteer accepts a position. In between the acceptance and onboarding phases, training materials coupled with opportunities to connect volunteers with supplemental subject matter should be provided. When coordinating volunteer projects, it is important to establish and share milestone dates to ensure everyone's attendance. Once you have approved a volunteer, and they accepted the position, it is important to promptly communicate those mandatory dates. Additionally, you should provide them with all the necessary materials and information, empowering them to prepare adequately for their new role.

It is vital to acknowledge that once you have booked time in a volunteer's schedule, you must honor and respect that commitment. Value your volunteers' time by recognizing that they have other responsibilities and commitments outside of their volunteer work. In the event of an unforeseen emergency that prevents their participation, it is important to have contingency plans in place. Having asynchronous training opportunities, an on-call volunteer pool, or having paid staff "backup" volunteers are some minor contingency plans. This will set volunteers up for continued success in their role, allowing them to navigate through any unexpected absences seamlessly.

A great way to encourage participation is to have a volunteer-only welcome series of emails. This can be conversational or something like a volunteer newsletter that gives insight and behind-the-scenes looks into what is going on at the museum. Newsletters and emails are a great way to drop in "Did you know?" facts and information. You can also add reading or show recommendations for anything upcoming that has relatable content for the volunteers. This bridges the time between being accepted into the volunteer group, their time spent going through the onboarding cycle, and the time they can start on their project. Each of these steps is important to keeping the volunteer interested, engaged, and excited about their new position at your museum.

Once a volunteer has completed their onboarding and general training, it is time to dig into their project. If their project requires specific training, it is important to get that scheduled and accomplished as part of their onboarding experience or shortly after their onboarding. As a volunteer coordinator, it is important that there is no gap between these two steps. You should be working with the volunteer supervisor (if you are not their project supervisor) to establish a project training schedule before the volunteer completes their onboarding with the museum. As you send your volunteers off to their projects, connect with them regularly to make sure they are getting the most out of their experiences.

Your role as the volunteer coordinator is not done as you send your volunteers off to their projects. One of the core functions of a volunteer coordinator is to cultivate a long-term relationship with your volunteer. Like a major donor to the organization, volunteers are investing their resources into the museum and its mission. It is important to nurture relationships with your volunteers for the long haul. You should maintain an open-door policy stating that any volunteer can come to you with needs and concerns at any time. We know sometimes an unexpected meeting with a volunteer may be inconvenient for your daily workload, but the relationship with your volunteer is, and should remain, your top priority.

Volunteers set to work with confidence they can complete the task at hand.
Image courtesy of the authors.

Relationships are essential to long-term success in your volunteer corps. Like donors, it is easier to keep a happy volunteer engaged than it is to find new volunteers who need to be interviewed, onboarded, trained, and guided through their first few experiences at your museum. With the support of your colleagues, you get to set the tone and work pace for your whole volunteer corps. You can make a volunteer's experience top-notch and keep them wanting to come back day after day, month after month, and even year after year.

TRAINING DAY(S) INTO THE FIRST THREE MONTHS

Joining a new organization can be an overwhelming time for a new volunteer. It is a time when the volunteer is meeting new people, learning new material, and getting familiar with a new building, site, and organization. As such, you should take the utmost care when planning and conducting training sessions for volunteers. Whether onboarding a new volunteer, training an existing museum stakeholder in a project, or supporting a regular volunteer in their growth and development, volunteer training sessions should be well thought out and logically organized. You should set clear objectives and expectations and create a timeline. This will help guide any trainee in their learning while preventing new volunteers from "burning out" before they get to engage in their project and blossom into thriving volunteers.

Scheduling volunteer training can seem overwhelming, and there is no one-size-fits-all approach. We will certainly give a few suggestions to help you make the most of the resources and opportunities you have ensuring that your volunteers start working on their projects as quickly as possible. For many small museums, volunteers tend to trickle in gradually, usually one or two at a time, as they become acquainted with your museum and find inspiration in its mission or connection to the community.

On the other hand, larger organizations often receive numerous applications for a single volunteer job posting and must adhere to a predetermined interview and onboarding process defined by their organization. As a volunteer coordinator, it is important to balance the needs of your organization while also providing support to your volunteers during the training process. This may require taking additional time to make sure that each volunteer can begin the process promptly and can successfully complete training. Many organizations hold monthly or quarterly volunteer meetings. All volunteer meetings are a great way to connect volunteers and get everyone on the same page with the information, policy changes, and training.

Oftentimes, the initial excitement for a volunteer wanes within a week if their schedule and early goals are not solidified right away. To ensure the sustained enthusiasm of volunteers, it is crucial to promptly engage them in onboarding and training after they express interest in your organization or project.

It is important to provide an engaging training program that takes advantage of this early enthusiasm.

When developing training, it is good to identify your goals for the training and identify how many sessions it will take to get through your material. After that, create an outline that covers all the information a volunteer will need to know. If the project requires the volunteers to have a special skill, it is important to integrate special skills learning or certification into your training schedule. For example, a cataloging project requires knowledge of authority records and standard vocabulary, while an event volunteer may be required to have first-aid certification.

Be sure to make a plan that is robust enough to ensure that the volunteer has all the basic information they need to get started, while still allowing for them to grow into their project and skills over time. This is also a great way to guarantee that training is timely and can be easily accomplished so that the volunteer can move on to their main project with your museum.

General goals for your volunteer training program may include the following:

- Volunteer is oriented to the building, galleries, project site, back of house, and digital platforms as needed.

Find opportunities to engage in training throughout the volunteer experience to build confidence in new skills.
Image courtesy of Wikimedia Commons.

- Volunteer has met project team, other volunteer colleagues, and staff.
- Volunteer knows where to take breaks, find resources, where to go in an emergency, how to contact volunteer coordinator/supervisor when needed.
- Volunteer is comfortable with their project and workstation/resources and supplies available to them.
- Volunteers know where to request resources to help them in their role at the museum.

The training outline you create will have both general organization information and policies that volunteers can reference, as well as specific information about the volunteer's position. A lot of volunteer coordinators like to create a volunteer handbook that is given to the volunteer on their first training day. In it, they can find the general information that you covered during training including museum hours and contact information for supervisors and other leaders at the museum. State whom your volunteers should contact when checking in, calling in sick, when a specific need arises, or when there is an emergency.

It can also include a section dedicated to the volunteer's specific project or role. For example, a tour guide may have the docent scripts, dress codes, and additional resources that will help them become more knowledgeable on frequently asked questions and general topical discussion in their handbook. A volunteer archives assistant may find basic subject headings, a collection processing step-by-step, and digitization specs helpful while an event volunteer may find event-specific info, dress codes, important information regarding visitor and donor stewardship, and bullet points for fostering engagement throughout the event important.

When developing your training sessions and volunteer manuals, it is important to consider how your volunteers learn, retain, and engage with information. As you have already had a welcome meeting with them, you should be able to have a good sense of any accommodations they may need such as large-printed documents, a digital version in a specific format for screen reading technology, or language interpretation. In museums today, it is not uncommon to rely on cloud-based storage to host much of the paperwork that we once printed out and hand-delivered at a training session. Having a virtual handbook is a great way to keep the document up to date and allow for quick additions.

While on-site training allows volunteers to connect directly with each other and the museum staff, virtual or online training can also be beneficial for many volunteers and organizations. Because the volunteer does not have to wait for another training session to be scheduled in order to start their volunteering at the museum, this style can be more engaging.

A few considerations are worth keeping in mind when creating virtual training resources. Chief among those considerations is that many volunteers like to have person-to-person contact with their colleagues; remember to keep options open for your volunteers to connect with you in real life as well as virtually. Other considerations for any virtual handbook or training may include helpful YouTube videos, websites, blogs, or social media pages to check out (and hyperlinked in your digital handbook). Last, provide an opportunity for volunteers to post questions or discussions, like a blog or forum, as other colleagues and volunteers may be able to answer questions or suggest resources for you in many instances, saving you time, and allowing for a stronger network to be built across your volunteer team.

When designing a virtual experience for your volunteers, especially early in their volunteer journey, make sure that your technology is accessible to multiple generations. We may take our fluency in googling, email, videoconferencing, and cloud-based files for granted, but many volunteers may struggle with technology or certain programs that rely on a skill set or natural ability some volunteers may not have. Although many can learn, adapt, and overcome, you want to make sure that your volunteer experience is topnotch, and having alternative platforms, access points to information, and easy troubleshooting guides will make all the difference to a new volunteer learning to navigate your museum's digital presence.

One of the best ways to provide virtual training to volunteers is through a closed website. Closed websites can be hosted on your organization's main website, as a secondary (child) site, or it can be one you create through a platform like Google, Wix, or WordPress. Closed sites may be as simple as Dropbox, Google Drive, or other cloud-based storage sites where you organize

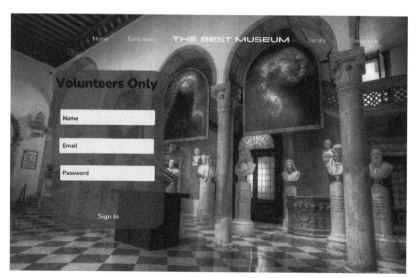

Closed websites are a great way to have resources available to volunteers whenever they need it.

Image courtesy of the authors.

your files for your volunteers to use and navigate. Find the best solution for your team by surveying those who will use the site most and gauge their comfort level navigating pages, cloud storage, and video hosting platforms.

You should advocate for a line in the training budget to pay for a page or host so that your volunteers can become generally self-sufficient in key areas. For example, general knowledge gathering, checking in with colleagues, asking project-specific questions, and other general points of interest can be accomplished with a closed website. This self-sufficiency with the general information about the museum and volunteering at the organization frees you up to plan special opportunities for your volunteers, check in with them one-on-one about their experiences, and foster deeper relationships across your team.

Generally, closed pages are not seen by the general public when they visit the museum's website and can generally be accessed by those who have been given a link and/or password to the site. The "train at home" or "volunteers only" site can contain general information about the organization and its history, collections, and programs, as well as schedules and calls for additional shifts or coverage, forms (word documents, fillable PDFs, or even web-based forms that can automatically track responses), and policies the volunteer may need to refer to during their work.

Here you also have an opportunity to create video training content that might include a virtual tour of spaces, how-to videos, and other lectures volunteers might find helpful for their role at the museum. You do not have to reinvent the wheel when it comes to online training content. Record in-person training sessions and upload them to your training site. You can also post general training videos from places like LinkedIn, that may focus on time management, how to use spreadsheets, or even unconscious bias. Use what is already out there, and then spend time and resources on creating training sessions unique to you and your museum.

Like all things digital there are free video hosting platforms like YouTube, or if you have a robust website, you can work with your information technology (IT) department to embed videos into a closed website. However, when creating virtual material, remember to include metadata in your PDFs, images, and videos as that will help visual description and other assistant programs read and open your material for a volunteer who depends on assistant technology. Additionally, it helps support more robust searching for all volunteers on your platform.

In the end, it is important to consider how your volunteers can connect with you, how they best learn new material, and how they want to retain information for the long term. It is important to consider how your technology and training materials are being received and used by your visitors. Can you make accessibility to the material easier and more inclusive? And most importantly you must allow for a space—in-person, virtual, or both—where volunteers can connect with each other, you, and museum colleagues throughout their onboarding and training experience.

BREAKING OUT ON THEIR OWN: THE VOLUNTEER JOURNEY

Since our first edition of *Recruiting and Managing Museum Volunteers*, we noticed that many museums learned that moving a volunteer from their training mode into their active and engaged "member of the team mode" is very challenging. We found this to be true in our roles as well. It is important to address some strategies that can assist in the success of our volunteers. It is crucial to provide them with the necessary support and resources to confidently tackle their new volunteer responsibilities with a mission to succeed at whatever you put in front of them.

By this point in the chapter, you will recognize the importance of a great onboarding and training experience. Too much and a volunteer could burn out before they even get to the gallery floor or the archive collection room; too little and they will get bored and look elsewhere to volunteer. With your onboarding process in place, you are up against your next big hurdle. Scheduling, timekeeping, and day-to-day management.

Like staff, it is important to keep track of the time volunteers are committing to the museum and what they are doing during their time. Some volunteers may have company match options (a cash gift to match their employees' volunteer hours) or students may need a letter of recommendation to continue their education, some health plans require confirmation of healthy living activities, and you will need to verify time and activities spent at the museum. Whatever the case may be, schedules, timekeeping, and activity tracking are essential to a well-run volunteer team.

So, where do we even start? Start with your schedule. For many museums, this can be a simple, but timely task. To schedule a volunteer's time well you need to understand the project(s) they are involved in, and the workflow or visitorship of the team they are working for. This is easy if you are a director, curator, volunteer coordinator, tour guide, or program manager; you know your needs and can quickly draw up a timetable for when you need someone the most to help you.

But if you are a larger organization, it is important to sit down with colleagues to create an active timetable and when it is best to have shifts covered by volunteers. A golden rule of thumb is to schedule volunteers for at least a three- or four-hour shift. This ensures that, generally, their commute is not longer than their shift. (You will often lose people if they spend more time in the car or on public transit than at the museum.) A four-hour shift will allow for the volunteer to potentially work with a change in staff, meet new people throughout their day, and accomplish an item or project (like inventory an archive box, or scan a small stack of pictures); leaving a job undone or at an unnatural breakpoint can frustrate volunteers if it happens frequently.

Once you have identified your ideal working times and determined the best duration for shifts, it is time to make up your schedule. Shifts can vary based on the project too. For example, an event greeter may wish to work a six-hour shift, whereas a concessions volunteer may need a break after a three-hour shift. We have found it easiest to make a timetable or chart on a blank page and fill in the blanks with your needs and volunteers. This can be posted in the museum and on the volunteer website with ease.

You can also create schedules through digital platforms and allow volunteers to sign up for shifts as they wish; however, a word of caution—many volunteers have the best of intentions but need to have someone to tell them when and where to be, especially early on in their volunteer journey. Do not be afraid to gather availability from your volunteers when you onboard them, but be in charge of scheduling their shifts for them.

It is also important to make sure you release your schedules well in advance of the first shift on that schedule. If people have a vacation planned, need to take off from another job, or have a conflicting commitment, the sooner you know, the easier it is to troubleshoot and the less guilty volunteers feel about having to miss a shift or reorganize their schedule.

When setting up a timekeeping system, it is best to have one central system that all volunteers use throughout the institution. Timekeeping systems can be as simple as handwritten timesheets in a binder or on a centrally located computer, up to managed timekeeping systems that allow volunteers to log in from workstations in the volunteer office, around the museum, or even from the volunteer's phone.

Remember that whatever your solution is for recordkeeping, you will want to make sure that all volunteers can access and use the system with minimal training and independently of you or other staff members. Regardless of what type of system a museum chooses to use, there is specific information all timesheets should include to help coordinators accurately capture a volunteer's hours and contributions to the organization. All timesheets should include the following:

- the volunteer's name and ID number
- the date and time the volunteer arrives
- the date and time the volunteer leaves
- the project or location where the volunteer worked during their time

A volunteer's ID, as well as the dates and times the volunteer worked, are obvious data captures for any volunteer manager to effectively schedule and recognize volunteers for their contributions to the museum. The location of work is important to know in the event of an emergency or if someone needs to get a hold of the volunteer. Places like historic sites may have many buildings spread across many acres, or a large encyclopedic museum may have hundreds of rooms where people work. A general collection area, gallery, or location helps responders, coordinators, and security staff know where people are throughout their site (especially if it is a remote room or building).

The project a volunteer is working on might also be important for funding applications, project development, and strategic planning, and for program and volunteer reviews. Knowing the skills and time your volunteers bring to the organization helps make a case for more resources to support your volunteer program, helps you contribute to future planning initiatives, and helps leadership establish a track record of community engagement for the museum's stakeholders and donors.

Having this critical task sorted out for your volunteer team is essential to a successful volunteer program. You should make schedules and timekeeping as easy and convenient for volunteers as possible to ensure accurate recording and reporting. By having accurate data, you help support the volunteer program and the ongoing operations of the museum.

Now that the volunteers are trained, scheduled, and clocked in, you get to sit back and watch their hard work and planning run like clockwork, right?

One-on-one conversations and small group sessions are great ways to keep up with volunteers and ensure that they are feeling great about their time at the museum.
Image courtesy of Wikimedia Commons.

Not exactly. Although we all hope that we have set our volunteers up for success, rarely do things take off smoothly and run uninterrupted. Now that our volunteers are out in the museum making a difference, we have to switch our focus from cultivation and training to stewardship and relationship building. It is during the first few months of the volunteer's experience that they become committed to the organization or not. This is where you have another crucial role to fill.

If you have done your training sessions well, volunteers are off to the races and excited about getting into their projects. Their project supervisors are also really excited to have the help and quickly set to work to get the project moving forward; however, this excitement to get things moving can sometimes have a detrimental effect on the long-term relationship with the volunteer.

Before sending the volunteer off to work with their project supervisor, take time to sit down with the supervisor and devise a strategy for the volunteer (or if you are their supervisor, take a minute to reconsider your mind-set). It is important to remember that volunteers, especially students and interns, require a fair bit of supervision during their first few months at the museum. The best-case scenarios allow for staff to work alongside the volunteer until they are completely comfortable with their project expectations and processes. If physical proximity is not possible (e.g., the volunteers are working on a remote or digital project), then make sure that you have an obvious, open line of communication and that the supervisor is checking in frequently on the volunteer and their project.

Training on project specifics can get intense for many volunteers. Like the general training and onboarding, there might be a lot of information coming fast to the volunteer (remember when we had to move all our computer files to "the cloud"? #stressful). It is important to check in after the volunteer gets some hands-on experience to make sure they feel properly trained and informed about their role. Tour guides may have memorized the tour script but found the flow of the tour awkward for them. As a volunteer coordinator, you might be able to suggest a different order of delivery to make it seem more natural for them. Or a collection intern may have learned a different cataloging nomenclature in school, and they are unsure of which authority files to use. As the project supervisor or volunteer coordinator, you can walk through the pros and cons of each system and decide how to proceed and where there are resources to help the intern be successful in knowing the authority files used at the museum.

Another example is event volunteers. There are times when volunteers are quickly trained and sent out to supervise a table or activity. But, in many cases, important museum stakeholders may arrive and participate in your event with their families or colleagues. If a fundraising staff member is not available to support the stakeholder's visit, a volunteer can step up with a little bit of training in donor stewardship, and even a few key stakeholders' history with the organization, to make sure the visitor has the best experience on site as possible.

As the first few months progress, and volunteers are working regularly, you will find they grow in comfort level with each shift. Troubleshooting questions become less frequent and volunteers start to express their ability to work while staff take a phone call, attend a meeting, or leave the site. As volunteers grow in confidence, it is okay to respect that transition and free staff time up for other important activities, but regular check-ins before, during, and after a volunteer's shift are important. Volunteers often become disengaged if they feel ignored or underappreciated in their efforts to support the museum's mission. So as they become more independent in their work, it becomes more crucial for staff to check in and tackle any questions, scout out interesting knowledge-expanding activities, and show gratitude and appreciation.

In general, three to four months of regular shifts can solidify the volunteer and their relationship with the museum. Celebrate this milestone with the volunteers and recognize their contributions with them and through your volunteer newsletter. (Do not forget to recognize annual or major project milestones too! More on that in the next chapter.)

This time out to recognize growth and contributions is especially meaningful to a volunteer if it was a hectic few months (like summer camp season) or transitional time (like a new traveling exhibition with programming came in) for your organization and the volunteer stepped in and really supported the organization through change.

In addition to recognizing the valuable contributions the volunteer made in their first few months, taking time to meet one-on-one with the volunteer and review their project and experience so far is one of the most important parts of managing any team in a professional capacity. Volunteer coordinators should regularly perform reviews with volunteers and on their projects in order to ensure that volunteers are contributing in a positive way to the institution and are having a positive experience in the process. Reviews provide an opportunity for

Recognizing a job well done is an easy way to keep volunteers engaged.
Image courtesy of Getty Images.

formal feedback that can be used for improving the volunteer's experience or project, providing recognition for the volunteer team, and facilitating external communications such as grants and reference letters if the need arises. During the one-on-one review with the volunteer, it is important to cover some basic information with a volunteer. Some items that should be covered in any review:

- Does the volunteer find the work too easy or too hard?
- Does the volunteer look forward to coming in, or do they dread the project and are only coming in because they committed to the project?
- Are there any special tools or training the volunteer needs?
- Does their volunteer schedule still work for them?
- And, for those on special projects, questions like "What type of project would you like next?" or "Would you like to continue at the museum with another project once this concludes?" are great ways to prepare for volunteer transitions and to encourage ongoing participation.

It is important for volunteer coordinators to make note of any issues that need follow-up, such as a request for supplies or additional training. Coordinators should also note whether the volunteer is looking for new volunteer opportunities and any changes in schedule or availability. All volunteer reviews should be documented and kept in the volunteer's file to reference in the future for recognition, training opportunities, and reference letters as they come up.

In addition to reviewing the volunteer, volunteer coordinators should facilitate evaluations for the volunteer to review the volunteer program, and anonymously if they so choose. This allows the volunteer to share their opinion about the organization, its mission, and its direction. The volunteer is invested in the museum, and their comments and concerns should be heard and acted upon when appropriate by museum staff and leadership. Volunteers have a unique perspective on how the community engages with and reflects upon the work of the museum and its relationship to its neighborhood and visitors.

CONNECTING WITH MUSEUM LEADERSHIP AND HIGHLIGHTING WORK

Throughout this chapter, you learned important strategies to welcome a volunteer onto your team and set them up for success at your museum. One area that is crucial to the success of a volunteer team but has yet to be addressed is the importance of reporting your work to leadership and other decision makers and stakeholders at the museum. As the advocate for your department and volunteer team, it is important to understand the basics of reporting and having data-driven results to present in staff meetings, funder meetings, and to the general public through publications like an annual report. Regardless of the way you are presenting your accomplishments and requesting needs, it is important to track your metrics deliberately and clearly.

There are three major sets of data that museum leadership is generally interested in collecting from its departments: (1) How does the program support the mission, vision, and goals of the organization? (2) What are the costs associated with accomplishing the *how*? (3) What can we do to improve the return on our investment (ROI) of the program? These reports become especially important during budget development for both the organization and projects specifically. If you can contribute to the dollars-and-cents conversation, you will ensure that your volunteers are able to contribute more to support the museum they love.

First, how does the volunteer program support the mission, vision, and goals of the museum? This one is important for situating your, and your volunteers,' work within the strategic operations of the museum. Consider collecting data that supports what projects are directly in line with the strategic goals of the organization. If a strategic goal includes acting as a guardian for community oral histories and artifacts from important historical events, a volunteer archive digitization project or cataloging project is essential to making the history of the community accessible to researchers and the public.

If a strategic goal is to increase donor engagement with the museum, volunteers serving during an event as hosts for donors help support the fundraising team with their donor stewardship strategy but leave the staff free to check in with multiple donors throughout the event without leaving an important donor unattended during the event. Other strategic goals may include public outreach, in-gallery programming, accessioning important pieces into the collection, or increasing funding to departments or research areas.

Volunteer support can be crucial to nearly every project or priority a museum has on the go. It is best to review the mission and strategic goals regularly and track what projects your volunteers are involved in as they relate to the mission and goals and be ready to present that information at a moment's notice.

Second, what are the costs associated with the volunteer department and projects? Don't you just love having to quantify workloads? Do not worry; although this can be an intimidating question to answer, many volunteer coordinators do this internally, and any coordinator or project lead must take some time to get numbers down on paper or in an easily refreshable report to send off to leadership. Executive directors and department heads lean on important numbers when they are speaking with funders and stakeholders. Having your numbers ready at all times ensures that those fundraising and advocating for the museum with external supporters are successful. The more you are prepared, the more your director will appreciate and understand what volunteers contribute to the museum.

So what do we need to track? There are all kinds of numbers to keep track of, which is why it gets overwhelming for some volunteer coordinators and department heads. The best way to get started on tracking your volunteers and their contributions to the museum is to create a spreadsheet and refresh

A simple rack card with important information and statistics will do the trick!

Image courtesy of the author.

it monthly or quarterly as your time allows. To show growth over time, it is sometimes helpful to track month to month and or year to year. Eventually, this helps identify trends in your volunteers and helps plan for future recruitment and recognition events. Here are some important areas to track for volunteer coordinators:

- Number of active volunteers (those who regularly work)
- Number of casual volunteers (some museums have a group of on-call volunteers, but they are not able or interested in committing to a regular schedule)
- Number of nonactive volunteers
- Number of hours per month (week or quarter) worked by volunteers
- Number (and type) of projects volunteers participate in
- Number of hours per month (week or quarter) dedicated to recruiting and training new volunteers
- Number of hours per month (week or quarter) dedicated to training and relationship building with current volunteers

Then there is some math to do (hence the recommendation to do this in a spreadsheet).

A. *Record the economic impact of volunteers (number of hours multiplied by volunteer salary figure equals economic impact for museum).*[1]
B. Sales or secured gifts in which volunteers were involved: for many organizations volunteers get up to 50 percent credit of cash brought in through securing donations or sales. Think of a volunteer working alongside one staff person at a raffle booth selling tickets, and they encourage families to buy a few extra tickets through their conversation—that volunteer should get credit for the funds raised at the table. Without them, the sales would have not been as successful. Track that sale!

    Most volunteer coordinators get the final totals of a fundraising campaign or event sales from their colleagues and divide the total by half to approximate the volunteers' contributions to fundraising.
C. *Track your time spent working directly with volunteers.* It is important to understand the economic impact of your work too.
D. *Track your expenses on supplies, training, and technology specific to volunteer management.* If you take your interpretive staff on a field trip training to another museum, track the mileage/travel, meals if any, admission, and other incidentals associated with the experience.

Third, what is your return on investment in your volunteer program? Ideally, a well-run volunteer team will have a higher economic impact than the coordinator's cost to support the volunteer team. If you have successfully tracked and calculated your important numbers, you can keep a running total of your ROI to give to any member of leadership who may need it. Simply put, your return on investment is the total of data points A and B (the contribution of the volunteer) above divided by C and D points (the museum investment in the volunteer) from above.

You should continuously reflect, adapt, evolve, and respond to changes in the organization and the community. By staying informed and proactive, volunteer coordinators can ensure that their programs remain supportive, robust, and aligned with the overall vision of the institution. Managing a team, or multiple teams of volunteers is a multifaceted responsibility that requires effective communication and continuous support. Throughout this chapter, we have explored the importance of supporting volunteers to ensure their success and meaningful contributions to your organization. By implementing the strategies and utilizing the tools presented in this chapter, volunteer coordinators can create a solid foundation for a thriving volunteer program that not only benefits the organization but also the volunteer.

NOTE

1. Independent Sector, "Independent Sector Releases New Value of Volunteer Time of $31.80 Per Hour," April 19, 2023, https://independentsector.org/blog/independent-sector-releases-new-value-of-volunteer-time-of-31-80-per-hour/#:~:text=(WASHINGTON%2C%20April%2019%2C%202023,6.2%20percent%20increase%20over%202021.

5

The Good and the Bad

MAINTAINING A TOP-NOTCH VOLUNTEER FORCE

In the last chapter, we explored the life cycle of a volunteer at an organization. We know that volunteers come to the organization with zeal and passion, and it is your responsibility to foster a deeper love and passion for the organization through the volunteer experience. But that is not always as easy as it sounds. It is important for you to anticipate challenges and have a troubleshooting plan in place while also looking for opportunities to celebrate your volunteers and their contributions. In this chapter, we will look at opportunities to recognize volunteers individually as well as celebrate with your whole team. We will also look at common challenges many volunteer coordinators face and explore effective ways to overcome those challenges effectively.

BUILDING TEAMS AND WORKING GROUPS

After successfully recruiting, onboarding, and training museum volunteers, the hard work begins! Like our own health, you will need to invest in your volunteer teams regularly to keep the team strong and functioning, while ensuring that your volunteers are comfortable with their responsibilities, are finding satisfaction in their roles, are successfully overcoming their challenges, and are engaging with colleagues in a meaningful and productive way. The key to a well-working volunteer team is a focus on inclusionary experiences and ongoing communication that focuses on relationship building across the team.

Like other team leaders throughout the museum, it is important to recognize opportunities to continually build ways for volunteers to connect with each other, learn about ways to engage in the museum, and allow the volunteers the opportunities to grow into their roles or explore other roles within the organization. As museums create more opportunities to provide access to their collections and to include more diverse groups including students, visitors, and community stakeholders, volunteers are a group of museum representatives

Building an inclusive team helps keep spirits up and conflicts to a minimum.
Image courtesy of Wikimedia Commons.

that can support and even lead initiatives that support new directives for accessibility and inclusionary experiences.

Ensuring that onboarding, training, and everyday practice are inclusive for all volunteers (and potential volunteers) is essential for creating a diverse and welcoming environment within the volunteer program. Creating a sense of welcome and belonging involves recognizing opportunities to build inclusion and equity throughout the volunteer corps. This can be done by actively seeking volunteers from diverse backgrounds, ensuring equal opportunities for participation in volunteer opportunities and supporting your volunteers' needs. The first step to increasing participation in your museum is to create a recruitment strategy that encourages underrepresented communities to become stakeholders and volunteers in your organization.

While you are recruiting new volunteers, you need to review your organization's policies and procedures and ensure that they support your organization's diversity, inclusion, and accessibility initiatives. This may include providing accommodations for volunteers with disabilities, offering resources and materials in multiple languages, and promoting a safe and respectful environment for all volunteers. Furthermore, you can encourage volunteers to share their perspectives and ideas on how to promote diversity and accessibility within the program and the organization at large. By valuing your volunteer input, you will create a culture of inclusivity where all voices are heard and respected. By incorporating training and recognizing opportunities to build inclusion and equality, you can foster a diverse and accessible volunteer program. This not only enhances the volunteer experience but also strengthens the museum's ability to provide inclusive and meaningful experiences for all visitors.

Diversity brings a range of perspectives, experiences, and expertise to your volunteer program. Each individual comes with a unique background, cultural understanding, and life experiences, which can greatly enrich the organization's activities and initiatives. A diverse volunteer group helps to create a welcoming and inclusive environment for all visitors. Visitors from different communities and demographics can better relate and connect with your museum and its objects. Having a diverse volunteer base can also attract visitors who may have previously felt excluded or underrepresented, bridging gaps and building strong connections with different communities. This fosters a sense of belonging and helps visitors feel represented, respected, and understood. Additionally, diversity within the volunteer group promotes learning and growth among the volunteers themselves.

By recognizing the importance of diversity, you can provide training sessions that educate staff and volunteers on the significance of inclusion and equality. These sessions can cover topics such as cultural sensitivity, understanding different abilities, and promoting accessibility in museum experiences. Interacting with individuals from different backgrounds helps volunteers develop empathy, cross-cultural communication skills, and a broader worldview. This not only benefits their personal growth but also equips them with valuable skills that can be applied in various aspects of their lives.

CELEBRATING SUCCESSES

The gift of time is the most valuable gift anyone can give to an organization. Unlike money or goods, time is the one thing people do not get (or make) back. Time is something that anyone, regardless of age or financial standing, can give to an organization and often that gift is filled with emotional investment in an outcome or experience. Because time is so valuable to everyone, it is important that your volunteers feel respected, needed, and appreciated at all times. Gratitude for a job well done is the key to a happy and successful volunteer program, and it is one of the best ways for you to connect with your volunteers as a group or on a one-on-one basis.

There are many ways you can show appreciation for volunteers. One way is to say a simple verbal thank you as a volunteer checks out for the day. Another way is to check in with them during their shifts to see if they need help or additional training. You can also organize elaborate volunteer parties and recognition gifts. The sky is the limit when it comes to volunteer recognition. The simplest way to recognize a job well done is to say "Thank you." All staff members and leadership should get into the habit of getting to know and thank every volunteer they see on campus. Thank you's can be a quick, verbal "Thanks for your time [hard work, or completing a project]" or thank-you notes left in a volunteer mailbox (or sent to their email or home address). If a volunteer regularly picks up extra shifts, goes above and beyond with a guest or project, or completes a special project, a handwritten thank-you note recognizing their contributions will make it clear that they are appreciated, which in turn will make them more apt to go above and beyond with the next guest or project.

A surprise thank-you note makes a volunteer's day.
Image courtesy of the authors.

RECOGNITION EVENTS

Planning and implementing recognition events play a vital role in volunteer management, alongside training and project management. These events not only contribute to the growth of your volunteer program but also help facilitate growth and foster the development of new volunteers. Although volunteer recognition events take more time and money than basic thank you's and pats on the back, they provide opportunities for the whole organization to come together to celebrate the accomplishments of not only your volunteers but also the organization as a whole. Because recognition events take more time and resources to plan, they are usually held once or twice a year, depending on resources and amount of volunteers. When starting out, organizations usually start with a summer, end-of-season, or holiday event. If the organization has a lot of volunteers or a lot of projects, multiple events can be planned throughout the year. These events are budgeted and planned for throughout the fiscal year, as they occur on an annual basis.

Big events, such as formal recognition dinners, usually take place off-site on an annual basis. These events are the big-budget events for the volunteer department, and all the stops are pulled for food, beverage, entertainment, and recognition gifts. With that said, even small organizations can throw great annual recognition parties when they are planned out and budgeted accordingly. In some communities, nonprofits will host other organizations' events for free or discounted charges. You can offer admission tickets, merchandise, or memberships for volunteer gifts from your museum, or partner with another community organization and trade benefits such as tickets to their museum. When hosting an annual recognition event, it is important to offer food and drink to the volunteers and their guests. To minimize the food and drink budget, museums sometimes serve canapés or hors d'oeuvres, provide a cash bar with complimentary nonalcoholic beverages, or host a brunch or dessert party.

Other recognition events can be as simple as monthly get-togethers with small lectures and potlucks, or as complex as group field trips to other museums or training sessions. Each of these events will show the organization's appreciation for the volunteers and their commitment to the museum. These events also provide an opportunity for you to provide additional training or learning opportunities for your volunteers. One type of recognition event is not better than the other, and these small events can be more budget friendly for a smaller organization or for those who would like to recognize their volunteers more often than once a year.

VOLUNTEER AWARDS AND GIFTS

No matter the size and budget of the event, the point of any recognition event is to thank the volunteers for their service and commitment to the museum. To reward the volunteers' hard work, you can create special thank-you gifts for volunteers who have reached milestones in hours worked or projects completed. Before any recognition event, you should tabulate the volunteer hours individually and note the total volunteer hours donated to the museum. This number can not only be used in funding appeals but also to encourage more volunteers to commit to more hours while highlighting individual contributions to the volunteer department. By highlighting individual contributions to the total hours contributed to the organization, your volunteers will feel like a part of a larger team and recognize the value they bring to the museum.

When you are ready to reward volunteers, it is important to choose rewards and gifts that are meaningful to them. Personal rewards, such as limited edition and branded coffee mugs, blankets, tote bags, and other souvenirs, allow museums to create a special gift for their volunteers. These awards should be awarded to individual volunteers based on any number of factors, including their commitment to the organization and commitment to continued training, the number of hours they provide to the museum, or the number of projects they completed over the year. Like offering donor gifts to those who give substantial financial support to an organization, rewarding those who donated a lot of time with special gifts helps make them feel appreciated, and recognition often inspires other volunteers to donate more time or participate in more projects. Friendly competition, especially among close friends and volunteer groups, is another way to actively engage people in an organization's volunteer program.

Volunteer recognition gifts should be included in the annual recognition budget, and new rewards can be developed every year. No matter the budget, there are many great options for museum volunteer gifts. Certificates of accomplishment and full memberships to the museum are an economical way for the museum to recognize the hard work and dedication of volunteers while saving some money, as both of these rewards can be produced in-house by museum staff. Other awards can range from gift shop vouchers or products to scholarships for classes, to tickets to other local museums or galleries, to raffle tickets for larger prizes offered once a year at the annual appreciation event. Regardless of the recognition gift, each item should be accompanied by a thank you, either verbal or, better yet, written and signed by the volunteer coordinator or supervisor and the museum's director or board president, as volunteers feel especially important when leadership takes time to acknowledge their contribution to the organization.

Planning and running recognition events are your responsibility; however, since volunteers serve all departments, other museum staff should be involved in preparation and execution. Department heads, coordinators, supervisors, and board members should all be invited to the event and offer to lend a hand as needed. Recognition events are all about the volunteers—rewarding and appreciating them for their time and devotion to the museum.

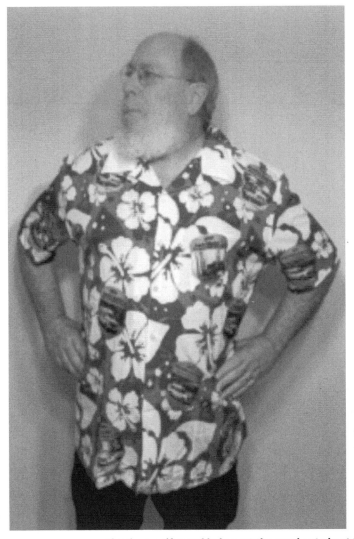

Museum swag can serve as thank-you gifts and helps get the word out about the great organization!

Image courtesy of Fred Claridge.

CONFRONTING CHALLENGES

Any time a group of people work together, differing opinions and personalities will inevitably cause tensions and even conflict among group members. Volunteer groups are not exempt from conflicting personalities and differing opinions. Sometimes, volunteers take such ownership of their projects they forget that there are other people involved in the project. They can also forget to report activities or decisions to you or their supervisors. Conversely, some volunteer coordinators assume that volunteers do not encounter any issues and sometimes ignore volunteers' need for help or suggestions for improvement or conflict resolution.

Although these conflicts happen in every organization, how conflicts and tense situations are handled can make or break the volunteer program. Communication is key to handling conflicts once they arise, and it can also prevent the escalation of conflict (or prevent conflict altogether) when basic strategies are implemented in a timely manner. The volunteer coordinator must be prepared to serve a human resource coordinator role as needed to mediate the best outcome for the volunteer and the organization during times of conflict.

Volunteers, like museum staff and leadership, should be held to the same standards of conduct and behavior. Like staff, volunteers go through a rigorous application process and take part in ongoing training to ensure quality and safety for the collections, visitors, and staff as well as the volunteers themselves. Volunteers are often the face of the museum during public events, guided tours, or even discussing their roles at the museum with friends and family. Like staff, if a certain volunteer (or group of volunteers) is being disruptive or insubordinate, or not representing the museum in a professional manner, you should act quickly to discuss the issue (or issues) with the volunteer and work to rectify the situation.

There are many steps you can take when addressing issues with volunteers. Prior to any corrective action, you should try to communicate with the volunteer to find out whether they are struggling with the project or whether any issues have arisen since starting their volunteer project. If a casual con-

Taking time to connect with a volunteer to discuss their challenges will help get the volunteer and team back on track.
Image courtesy of small-improvements.com.

versation with the volunteer does not yield results or a change in behavior, the following protocol will help you work toward a beneficial solution to most, if not all, issues that arise.

The first step is to document issues that you observe or document the issues that are reported to you by staff or other volunteers and visitors. Documenting issues in writing allows you to address specific instances when having conversations or training sessions with the offending volunteer. After documentation, sit down with the volunteer or volunteers and have a candid conversation about the roles and expectations of the organization and the volunteer(s). In some cases, the issue may be as simple as a miscommunication or a lack of training in the problem area.

During these conversations, you may want to discuss how the volunteer's behavior is affecting the workplace or visitors. Be sure to discuss steps they can take to come to a positive solution to the problem. More often than not, a simple review of procedures or additional training is all that is necessary to solve issues that arise in volunteer groups. If necessary, you can prepare a document that outlines the steps they agree to take and a date to follow up to review the steps and address any other issues that arise. Both, or all, parties involved can sign these documents.

Risk and Opportunity Log

Volunteer name:				
Date	Objective at Risk	Description of Risk	Agreed upon Action	Volunteer Signature & Volunteer Coordinator Signature

Risk and Opportunity Log.
Image courtesy of the authors.

Another way you can engage volunteers in modifying their behavior before corrective action is the development and posting of opportunity and risk logs (also referred to as O&R logs). These logs are a positive tool used to modify negative behavior and are created with the input of the offending party and their supervisor and volunteer coordinator. O&R logs are structured in a way to outline which museum objectives are at risk, what behavior is causing that risk, and what actions can be taken to eliminate the risk.

When filling out the O&R log, identify what institutional objective is at risk. This should be an easy question to answer, as it is generally the issue that is brought to your attention. Is a volunteer giving incorrect information in a gallery? Are they handling artifacts without the proper precautions? Have they been rude and abrasive to fellow volunteers, staff, or visitors? Together you and the offending volunteer can review how their behavior is affecting the museum.

Asking the volunteer how they think their actions are affecting the highlighted objective or issue is a great way to start a conversation with the volunteer and hear their side of the story. Recording their input to the situation in your notes helps the volunteer understand how their actions are perceived by others and what effect they are having on the organization. The conversation should also address the consequences of these behaviors, and you should discuss actions to modify the problematic behavior that will be documented in the O&R log. After documenting the issues and follow-up actions, you should make sure the volunteer understands the situation and the part they will play in solving the situation.

Finally, there is a section in the O&R log for both parties to sign, signifying that the volunteer understands and will work toward solving the initial problem and that you, and/or the volunteer supervisor, will provide the necessary training and professional support to make the volunteer successful. This log, or a record of the meeting, should go into the volunteer's file, in addition to any other documentation discussed during the conflict-resolution meeting.

NO-CALL AND NO-SHOW VOLUNTEERS

Richard Weingardt put it best when he said, "The world is run by those who show up."[1] So what happens when a volunteer does not show up for a shift or training session? Many for-profit businesses use a "no call/no show" policy. This means if an employee fails to show up, disciplinary action takes place. Volunteers should be held to the same accountability as paid staff; however, sometimes volunteers do not realize their impact when they do not show up for a shift or program. The connotation of the word *volunteer* might evoke a carefree attitude to new volunteers, especially if this is their first volunteer position. They may assume that if they are giving their time freely, they can come in as they feel like it and not show up if other activities arise. Many new volunteers sometimes feel that missing a shift or event would not matter that much to the department or organization.

From the beginning, you and the rest of the museum staff should work to correct the idea that an organization is not dependent on a volunteer. The best way to do that is to explain how the volunteer's job or duty directly affects the museum, its staff, and visitors. Some volunteer coordinators are passive when bringing on new volunteers as they do not want to scare the potential volunteer off; as a result, the volunteer coordinator may make out some of the duties or responsibilities as less important than staff projects. However, it is important that *you* do not fall into this trap, and you should strive to make every volunteer job seem important to the organization.

From the very beginning, a potential volunteer should know their expectations and goals, and how their accomplishments are measured. If a volunteer feels that their job is important and integral to the success of the program and organization, they are more likely to take the position seriously. Addressing 1,500 membership letters might seem like busy work, but if you can explain how that action fits into the big picture—increased membership renewals and helping the museum achieve its annual budget—the volunteers will have more pride in their work and be more apt to communicate changes in schedules and availability.

On occasion, a volunteer may forget a shift (especially when it is on an irregular time or date) or simply lose track of days during the week. When irregular no-shows happen, you or the volunteer's supervisor should call or email

Some volunteers may forget about their shift or chose not to come. A strong team will carry on, but be sure to address the issue with your volunteer to ensure they are okay and able to continue.

Image courtesy of the authors.

The Good and the Bad

the volunteer to check in. In some cases, a person may have fallen ill or had a family emergency, and they simply forgot to call. As mentioned before, some may simply lose track of time, especially during summer vacations or during the holiday seasons. In certain instances, your volunteer may be incapacitated or injured and alone at home. You may be the only person to check in, and potentially save a life. In these cases, a simple check-up call is all that is needed, and in many cases, the volunteer will be very apologetic and want to confirm their next shift.

In most cases, a volunteer will work hard to prevent another no-show shift, and no other corrective action is needed. However, some volunteers may not keep to a regular schedule and have a problem maintaining their attendance. In these cases, more corrective action will need to take place. If you have met with the volunteer to stress their importance to the organization and the volunteer continues to not show up or not adhere to their schedule, the O&R log and the subsequent meeting should be the next steps in resolving the issue.

Like other conflicts that arise, if a volunteer is unable to maintain a working schedule with the museum, a volunteer coordinator may be forced to relieve the volunteer of their duties or place them in another department that suits their schedule. It is important to remember that as valued as volunteers are in an organization, when it comes to enforcing rules and expectations, the organization's best interests should be the number-one priority and you should feel empowered to do what you need to for the health of the organization.

ROGUE VOLUNTEERS

In a perfect world, the first conflict-resolution meeting is enough to help the volunteer recognize the issue at hand and change their behavior accordingly. In fact, many times a simple meeting and follow-up is all that is needed to resolve issues with volunteers. However, there may come a time when a volunteer does not change or a bigger problem develops as a result of the first conflict resolution meeting. Many museums call these *rouge volunteers*.

When faced with a rogue volunteer, you or the volunteer's supervisor should use the same O&R log that documented the previous infraction(s). You *should* be empowered to take the same steps as before, but this time find out why the agreed-upon actions did not work. Conflict-resolution meetings can be very emotional, and it is important for you to keep your emotions in check while working with volunteers so that you can help find solutions to what can be very personal problems. In many cases, volunteers have external factors affecting their abilities to volunteer. If you are comfortable doing so, you can offer suggestions for resources for help, based on the volunteer's needs. However, in rare cases, a volunteer is unable to modify their behavior in an appropriate amount of time, if at all. If after three conflict-resolution meetings, a volunteer is still having issues, it is best for the organization to relieve them of their duties.

When faced with a third or even fourth meeting, depending on your volunteer policies, you should take time to meet with the volunteer and let the offending party know that the original issue has not been resolved despite the previous attempts to reach amicable solutions. Again, the O&R log comes in handy to illustrate issues that have been addressed and the agreed-upon follow-up actions. At this point, it is good to ask the volunteer if they understand the issue and actions that were documented during previous meetings.

In a majority of issues, the volunteer may simply not be able to perform a task or may feel uncomfortable in their current team, and could be too embarrassed to admit how they are feeling. You can encourage volunteers to accept a reassignment, or new project, in hopes of alleviating the issues at hand. Removing or firing a volunteer from the institution altogether is the last action a museum should take in resolving conflicts.

Volunteers give their time, and in many cases money, to the organization because they agree with the mission and want to support the museum to the best of their ability. Efforts should be made to retain any volunteers who have dedicated significant time before the incident at hand. Previous commitments and any promises of gifts, however, should not automatically ensure a volunteer's continued involvement with your museum. Despite their best intentions, some volunteers simply do not work out, and poor performance or bad behavior can hurt the activities and mission of the museum if not dealt with appropriately and in a timely fashion.

Volunteer teams often encounter several common challenges. In this chapter, we have provided standard approaches to address these challenges. However, it is important to ensure that any policies and procedures that are implemented are aligned with your organization's human resources and leadership guidelines. The following examples highlight common issues with volunteers and provide effective strategies to combat and troubleshoot them.

ISSUE: Time or shift management

EXAMPLES: No call/no shows, consistently late, chronic short-shifters

How to combat: To combat volunteers who have poor time management, several strategies can be implemented. You can conduct one-on-one conversations with the volunteers to help identify the root causes of their time-management issues. By understanding their needs for leaving early or coming late, coordinators can work toward finding solutions that accommodate their schedules while ensuring the necessary coverage for shifts.

Another approach is to reassess and reconfigure the schedule to better match the availability and preferences of the volunteers. This can help reduce instances of no-shows, lateness, and chronic short-shifting. You can also consider if there are any physical or mental barriers that may hinder volunteers from fulfilling their shift responsibilities and responding to those needs as necessary.

By addressing and working to overcome these barriers, you can help volunteers improve their time-management skills. Overall, open communication, schedule adjustments, and addressing any barriers can help combat time-management issues among volunteers and improve their reliability and consistency in fulfilling their commitments.

ISSUE: Going "off-script"

EXAMPLES: Inaccurate information, ghosts, conspiracy theories, alternate histories

How to combat: To combat volunteers going off-script or giving wrong information to guests, it is crucial to provide comprehensive training. This includes developing a detailed training program that covers all the necessary information your volunteers need to know about your organization, its mission, values, and the correct information they should provide to guests. Clear guidelines should be communicated, emphasizing the importance of sticking to the designated script and providing accurate information.

Role-playing exercises during training sessions can help volunteers practice responding to different scenarios while staying on script. Regular updates, ongoing supervision, and feedback can ensure volunteers are aware of any changes and provide constructive guidance. Peer mentoring can pair new volunteers with experienced ones to learn from their understanding of the script. Encouraging questions and open communication creates an environment where volunteers can seek clarification if unsure about any information. By implementing these strategies, you can combat volunteers going off-script or providing wrong information to guests.

ISSUE: Property destruction, broken materials, damaged collections

EXAMPLES: Lack of care with materials and collections, and sometimes serious, yet innocent mistakes can ruin artifacts or collections

How to combat: When a volunteer is involved in property destruction, it is essential to address the issue promptly and determine whether it was intentional or accidental. If the destruction was nonmalicious but resulted from a lack of care or innocent mistakes, consider reassigning the volunteer to a different role that aligns better with their skills and abilities. Provide additional training, clear guidelines, and close supervision to prevent similar incidents in the future.

However, if the destruction was intentional, take appropriate disciplinary measures and, if necessary, involve the authorities. By taking proactive steps and implementing stronger oversight, you can combat property destruction caused by volunteers and protect their collections and materials.

ISSUE: Theft

EXAMPLES: Excessive resource use, missing items, unauthorized deaccessioning/throwing away material

How to combat: To combat theft, organizations should establish clear documentation and policies regarding the proper use of resources. This involves creating guidelines on resource allocation, such as limiting the number of copies that can be made on a copier or designating authorized personnel to handle specific equipment. By documenting these procedures and regularly reminding volunteers of their responsibilities, you can make sure that resources are used appropriately and minimize the risk of theft.

Maintaining a comprehensive inventory of physical items and conducting regular audits can help to monitor their whereabouts and identify any missing items promptly. By securely storing donor logs and restricting access to authorized personnel, organizations can also protect sensitive information and reduce the risk of data theft. In summary, combating theft involves effective documentation and policy implementation.

Establishing clear guidelines for resource usage and regularly reminding volunteers of their responsibilities are essential. Additionally, maintaining a comprehensive inventory, conducting regular audits, and securely storing sensitive information can help organizations safeguard their resources and protect against theft. If you do encounter a theft, contact the proper authorities.

ISSUE: Disrespectful/threatening behavior

EXAMPLES: Infighting between volunteers and other volunteers and staff. Issues with volunteers and public

How to combat: When volunteers display disrespectful, rude, threatening, or even physical behavior toward each other, it is time to take immediate action to address the situation. The first step is to have a clear policy in place that outlines expected behavior and consequences for any violations. This policy should be communicated to all volunteers during their training and orientation.

To combat disrespectful behavior, you should establish a system for reporting incidents and encourage volunteers to come forward with any concerns or complaints. When an issue arises, it is important to address it promptly and confidentially. This may involve conducting private meetings with the individuals involved to discuss the behavior, remind them of the organization's policies, and provide an opportunity for them to express their concerns. Mediation or conflict resolution sessions can be arranged if necessary to help resolve conflicts between volunteers or between volunteers and staff.

If the behavior escalates to physical violence or poses a serious threat, involving external authorities becomes essential. In such cases, you or the volunteer's supervisor should immediately contact the police to ensure the safety of everyone involved. Legal counsel should also be sought to understand potential liability and to provide guidance on handling the situation appropriately.

Additionally, notifying your museum's insurance company is crucial to address any potential claims or damages resulting from the incident. Overall, combating disrespectful, rude, threatening, or physical behavior among volunteers requires a proactive approach, including clear policies, confidential reporting systems, prompt intervention, and involving external authorities and resources when necessary to ensure the safety and well-being of all individuals involved.

If you are new in your position or starting a new volunteer program, your organization may not have set policies in place. A common challenge faced by volunteer coordinators is the absence of established policies and procedures.

Volunteer Onboarding Manual

A Comprehensive Guide to a successful volunteer experience

2024 EDITION

Cover of Onboarding Manual.
Image courtesy of the authors.

To address this, it is time for you to write them! To start, you can use policies already established by your human resources team and modify them for volunteer purposes. You can also take any of the examples above and create policies around them, or any other issues that you foresee happening.

By ensuring that all volunteers have access to policies that affect them and their volunteer role, you can prevent misunderstandings and differentiate between minor issues and more serious situations. Providing volunteers with necessary information, guidelines, and corrective measures allows them to thrive and contribute effectively.

SAYING GOOD-BYE

Saying good-bye to a volunteer is never an easy task, especially when they have generously dedicated their time to your museum. However, there are instances when parting ways becomes necessary, such as when a volunteer demonstrates resistance to training and correction. In such cases, holding on to them can result in wasted time, strained relationships, and even potential damage to your museum.

It is also important to recognize that volunteers have their own natural end to their time at the museum, whether it be the completion of a project or their pursuit of new adventures. This section focused on handling the departure of volunteers, including assisting in finding new opportunities both within and outside the museum. Additionally, it offered guidance on gracefully letting volunteers go when the fit is not right and ensuring a smooth transition for the rest of the team after someone leaves.

Our hope is that if you follow the principles already addressed in this book and maintain clear communication and expectations, it is unlikely that a volunteer will ever reach a point where they become disgruntled. It is always good to be prepared for any exception and situation. Even with the best of intentions, people can become frustrated and have negative experiences. Emotions tend to run high, and the more emotion invested in a situation the harder it will be to have a calm, critical conversation. It is your job to navigate situations and prevent them from escalating as much as possible.

Alas, some coordinators find they have an escalating situation that they cannot control, despite their best efforts. In many cases, volunteers have become so frustrated that they can make unreasonable demands or threats against the organization. It is important to not take any conversations at this level personally and to maintain a professional demeanor. In many, if not all, cases, senior leadership should be involved in conversations with the volunteer at this point.

Having multiple people involved in these situations will demonstrate to the volunteer that you are not alone in the policies they are enforcing; in addition, multiple people can create incident reports that may be used if legal action is taken against the museum. The idea of legal action can be scary to museum leadership, but there are simple steps that can be taken to ensure that the organization is properly prepared for such an event.

After you have exhausted all avenues, including open communication, conflict resolution, and extra training, it may be best for the organization and volunteer to part ways. The exit of a volunteer should be dealt with as professionally as taking them on. The first step is to schedule a meeting with the volunteer. Other senior staff can also be invited, including the volunteer's supervisor, the human resources director, or even the executive director.

Regardless of who is sitting in the meeting, you should lead the meeting with the volunteer in question. The invited senior staff should not interject or add their "two cents," unless you or the volunteer invite them to join the conversation. Their main job is to be a witness to the meeting and help document the meeting when necessary.

Prior to the meeting, you should be prepared with any paperwork or write-ups that pertain to the volunteer. They should also have talking points prepared so that you can address all issues that need to be addressed. It is important to stay on task and not get distracted by pleading or other unpleasant happenings that could occur during the meeting. You should present the reasons for termination to the volunteer in written form. It is a good idea to go over it with the volunteer, point by point if necessary, and both of you sign it after the conversation. It is also important to clearly explain that they are relieved of their duties and essentially terminated as of a predetermined date. This is not a place to be ambiguous. This is also a time to retrieve any of the museum's materials, such as keys, uniforms, name tags, or volunteer membership cards.

During the whole process, it is important for all involved to be empathetic, caring, and honest; after all, the volunteer did provide services to the museum, and they should still feel respected by the organization, regardless of the reasons for leaving. The volunteer remains a member of the community, and any hard feelings that the volunteer leaves with could be detrimental to the standing of the organization.

When volunteers join your museum, they generally do so with enthusiasm and passion. As a volunteer coordinator, it is your responsibility to foster a deeper love and passion for the museum and its mission through the volunteer experience. Any volunteer coordinator will experience the highs and lows that come with working in diverse teams with many projects and personalities, your journey will be no different. We know that this task is not always simple, but we also know you are equipped to create rewarding experiences, address challenges, and support volunteers as they transition in and out of your team and organization.

This chapter serves as a guide for you to enhance the volunteer experience and establish a diverse, inclusive sustainable volunteer program at any museum. In the next section, we present a series of special chapters followed

Volunteers Celebrate at an Annual Volunteer Luncheon.
Image courtesy of the authors.

by a series of case studies relating to specific areas of volunteerism that have spurred conversations in the museum field and how best museum coordinators can support these specific activities as volunteers get involved.

NOTE

1. Richard Weingardt, "Leadership: The World Is Run by Those Who Show Up," *Journal of Management in Engineering* 13, no. 4 (1997): 61–66.

Part II

Special
Considerations
for Special Groups
of Volunteers

6

Utilizing Volunteers in Development and Resource Acquisition

Volunteers can put the FUN in fundraising! With a little bit of know-how, a pinch of planning, and a lot of teamwork, many volunteers can turn into incredible development partners, board members, and frontline fundraisers; they just need the chance and your support to thrive. This chapter is especially for small museums and volunteer-led organizations who are struggling with initiating meaningful and sustainable fundraising plans or building the confidence to take their mission to donors and funding partners in their community. We hope to provide an introduction into thinking about fundraising for your museum and ways volunteers can actively fundraise, support donor stewardship, and help secure necessary resources for any organization.

Museums, galleries, and other nonprofits rely on in-kind and monetary gifts to keep buildings open and the organization operating smoothly. In our experience, there are two common fallacies among museum leadership when it comes to volunteers and fundraising:

1. *Fundraising is solely a staff member's job.* When in actuality one of the most common volunteer jobs in America is fundraising for an event or organization; think of all the cookies and candy that get sold for groups annually! Why should museums let scouts and sports teams have all the fun?
2. *Asking volunteers for donations or asking them to help raise funds for the museum is negating the gift of time they are already donating.* According to VolunteerHub, 66 percent of volunteers are more likely to become financial donors than other museum stakeholders and are just as likely to be long-term, legacy, or recurring as volunteers who have an in-depth knowledge of the organization and its needs, almost in real-time.[1] Volunteers are more likely to share personal experiences about an organization they volunteer with, compared to the average visitor. They share these experiences with their friends and family, on social media, and with coworkers. And, both volunteers and visitors are more likely to share their experiences of an organization than community members who have not been engaged

with the museum at all. It goes to show how important it is to have engaged volunteers involved in creating a strong sense of community around museums. All this to say volunteers are an amazing tool in any fundraiser's toolbox. But like other volunteer opportunities, a solid plan and attainable goals are essential to success.

THE DONOR-VOLUNTEER

Volunteers have many pathways to your organization. Some may have visited and were inspired by your museum's mission, collections, or events. Some may have attended a program or chaperoned their child's field trip and connected with staff, subject matter, or the galleries and space. Some volunteers may be donors, who have given to the organization financially and are now able to commit some time to support the museum in additional ways.

These donor-volunteers are a unique group of individuals who value the organization enough to dedicate financial resources as well as their time. By welcoming them into your volunteer corps, you are joining your colleagues in the fundraising department to extend a special stewardship opportunity, allowing these donors to connect more deeply with the organization they care about.

For many donor-volunteers, they will come to the volunteer program with knowledge about your organization. They may have special projects or interests in mind, and in some cases, those may be reflective of their financial contributions. Like other volunteers, it is important to go through the same application, onboarding, and training process. It may be tempting to skip this process,

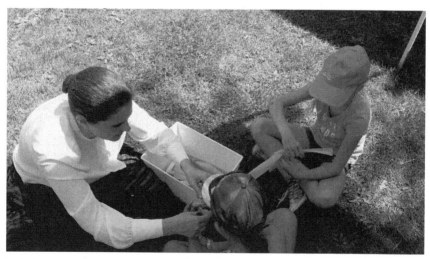

Volunteers are frontline representatives who build relationships with new stakeholders through programs and events.
Image courtesy of the authors.

especially if the potential volunteer is already familiar with the museum, staff, and leadership. Leaders may also be spearheading the "skip-the-line" approach to woo select stakeholders with opportunities to get more involved with the museum. Stick to the process and fall back on your policies and procedures whenever you need to make your case. These introductory steps allow you to get to know the volunteer, assess their interests, and allow them to understand the needs of the organization and the procedures of the volunteer department.

If the volunteer is a major donor, someone on your development team is probably assigned to be their point of contact (usually called a relationship manager), and you will want to work closely with that person to support the donor-volunteer through their transition into volunteering. Additional pressure may be felt when welcoming a donor-volunteer onto your team, as the volunteer experience may now be tied to a financial gift to the museum. This is when sound practice and lots of opportunities to connect and grow as a team allow your volunteer to express their interests and concerns to you about the museum.

Care should be taken to follow up on any issues and be sure to check in with the volunteer's development relationship manager or other development colleagues regularly if troubleshooting an issue is necessary. Just like with other volunteers, taking moments to connect, address concerns, and share information across teams helps to ensure that trust and appreciation are felt by all. Together you, the donor-volunteers' project supervisor, and the development team can provide a wonderful experience for the volunteer to continue to experience the impact of their gifts at the organization in many ways.

VOLUNTEERS TURNED DONORS

Donors who become volunteers often do so because they have a deep passion for the organization and wish to contribute in a more hands-on way. Like donors, volunteers who are passionate about the museum can decide to financially support the museum or special projects. These dedicated individuals may express their interest in making financial commitments or even donating collection items to the organization in which they volunteer. It is a testament to their commitment and the strong connection they feel for the mission of your museum. As a volunteer coordinator, you can facilitate introductions to your development team and, in the instance of collection material, to the curators or archivists at the museum to help the volunteer explore their interests in giving to the museum.

One of the easiest ways volunteers donate is through one-time or recurring gifts. Small cash gifts made online, at the admissions desk, or through their bank or employer to general funds or a special project may help volunteers feel more connected with the museum. This type of giving is usually initiated by the volunteer on their own or through a peer asking for a donation. As a volunteer coordinator, you may want to work with your development colleagues to ensure they know which of their donors are also volunteers and coordinate special recognition throughout the year. Additionally, it may be beneficial to work with your development department to create different templates that acknowledge their gift of time.

In the same vein as a small cash gift, some volunteers enjoy being members of the museum in which they work. Museums sometimes encourage volunteers to become members by offering discounts or even a free membership to volunteers if a minimum amount of hours are served annually. These benefits can also be used as recruitment tools. Although this idea has changed in some organizations, many house museums and other small organizations find it helpful to offer opportunities for members and volunteers to connect and share their passion for the museum together. Bringing members and volunteers together builds peer-to-peer relationships ultimately allowing more donors to learn about volunteer opportunities and how they can get more involved. This also allows volunteers to hear from donors expressing what they enjoy most

Volunteers can be avid collectors and may choose to donate their personal collection to the museum. Managing expectations early helps the volunteer feel appreciated no matter the donation outcome.
Image courtesy of the authors.

about the museum and the experiences the volunteers often create for visitors throughout the site.

Gifts-in-kind and gifts to the collection can be another way volunteers can expand their giving to their museum. These gifts require careful planning and a little bit of foresight to avoid unwanted situations. Receiving donations that your museum cannot utilize or turning a volunteer's collection gift away because it does not fit in the collection scope are instances that you can avoid with donation policies. The disappointment a volunteer may feel after having their gift rejected can be overcome by connecting early on in the process, before the volunteer has purchased supplies or has decided to gift material to the museum's collection.

More often than not volunteers, if they have been through your awesome onboarding sessions and have a strong relationship with you and others in the museum, know to approach you or a collection manager or museum leadership before initiating any gift to the museum. As a volunteer coordinator, you can facilitate these early conversations by keeping up with your volunteer and their activities at the museum and milestone moments in their lives. Try not to overpromise anything to your volunteer. The decision to accept a donation may not lie with you. Saying "yes" without the authority may leave you having to backtrack, or worse, disappoint the volunteer.

If you are a part of the event-planning team and a volunteer offers to make an event supply run to the local discount store, it is important to make sure that the volunteer and staff know exactly what supplies the volunteer will be picking up, and if they will be donating the supplies or expecting reimbursement. If there are a lot of supply needs, additional volunteers can help by shopping other supply lists, or the museum can prepare and effectively spend its budget on the remaining supplies. The worst outcome though is having so many extra supplies that a volunteer stash may not be used. This may make the volunteer feel like their efforts were in vain. Keeping lists, delegating tasks, and ensuring tasks are divided evenly will keep everyone's expectations and efforts aligned.

Collection material donations can be a harder conversation to have with volunteers. Although every museum is subject to a volunteer finding, purchasing, or having a unique piece of art or collection of photographs or personal patterns of interest, many volunteers can become emotionally invested in the museum and the material they think the museum needs or the items they want the museum to have for the collections. If a volunteer's donation is accepted into the museum's collection, volunteer coordinators, along with curators, collection management staff, and development officers, have to coordinate efforts to ensure that the volunteer is supported through the donation process. If their items were declined, this team should ensure that the volunteer had a positive experience throughout and is still excited and engaged with the museum, its mission, and its activities.

The last major area where volunteers are likely to turn into donors is through their estate planning and legacy-giving. No two legacy-giving programs look exactly alike, but some common threads are leaving a gift to a museum through the direct transfer of assets or cash originating in an estate or trust, through directives of a certified will, or through family members upon a settlement of an estate. In most cases, these gifts are made posthumously after careful consideration between the donor and their families, friends, and lawyers. Each gift is very personal for the donor and for their family. Special care should be taken to recognize the legacy gift whenever possible.

It is common practice for organizations to recognize donors who have made a legacy gift commitment. Some organizations do not have the infrastructure to support special clubs for identified legacy givers. In the same vein, some legacy givers chose not to disclose their legacy intentions while others happily share their intentions for their estate. For volunteers, the variety of givers mirrors that of the general public. However, as mentioned earlier in this chapter, because of their close connection to the organization, many volunteers, especially long-term volunteers, feel special to the organization and are likely to have some note in their estate plan to involve the organization in their legacy giving.

As a volunteer coordinator, this is an exciting opportunity to connect and partner with your development team. As an advocate for your volunteer, you will support the long-term conversations that help volunteers recognize how their legacy will continue on at the museum through their work as a volunteer and through their gifts to the museum. You, along with development colleagues, if they are able, can honor volunteers who have left legacy gifts in the past and who are committed to leaving gifts in the future. By publicly recognizing those who have made a legacy gift commitment to your organization, you provide an opportunity for other volunteers to recognize and appreciate their contributions. This recognition also creates a space for volunteer groups to engage in conversations and delve into the idea of leaving their own legacy gifts. Allowing volunteers to naturally explore the concept of legacy giving is a simple yet impactful way to support them through this avenue of giving.

In short, working closely with leadership, development, and other departments to both understand the needs of the organization and connect interested volunteers to the appropriate channel helps any volunteer coordinator connect more deeply with their volunteers and helps foster more engaging and positive relationships with departments and volunteers for the good of the organization's future.

FUNDRAISING WITH VOLUNTEERS

Fundraising can provide an exhilarating opportunity to work with volunteers and garner unique perspectives from a diverse group of museum stakeholders.

There are mixed feelings among museum leadership and professional fundraisers regarding volunteers and making *the ask*. Our intention with this section is to introduce ways that volunteers can support fundraising staff, if and when there is interest. Additionally, we wanted to share ways that small volunteer-run organizations can get into fundraising in a positive way. Volunteers are more likely to reflect the communities your museum serves than the staff. Traditionally, development officers have faced challenges in diversifying their staff and experiences to align with the museum's mission, vision, and values. While certain museums have made significant progress, others continue to struggle due to factors such as their location or the limited applicant pool for various positions.

Volunteers who are interested in the business side of museums, specifically in finding or securing sustainable funding, can play an important role in complementing development staff in small- and medium-sized organizations. Additionally, they can provide support to large organizations as they explore new communities to establish meaningful relationships. Through this section we will look at a few opportunities where volunteers can get engaged with donor stewardship, supporting development teams with some of their tasks in donor cultivation, and yes, even exploring opportunities where volunteers can help make *the ask*.

We will reference volunteer board activities as part of this section briefly, but it may also be helpful to reference the next chapter on engaging and supporting volunteer boards and how to support their work to more robustly understand how a volunteer coordinator and volunteer corps can help ensure financial sustainability for the museum they care about. Before any fundraising activities are taken on by volunteers or staff, it is important to have a fundraising plan and gift policies in place so that they can be leaned on when necessary and help keep the development team—whether it is board, staff, or volunteers—on the same page.

If you have volunteers embarking on fundraising efforts, it is essential to invest time in connecting with the fundraising individuals or teams within your museum. By establishing this connection, you can gain a better understanding of the expectations for volunteers, in terms of support, activities, and methods. Moreover, clarifying what is not expected from volunteers and making sure that they have clarity on their roles and responsibilities will make you a better advocate for your volunteers' expectations and needs. Knowing a little bit about how your fundraising department functions will go a long way in your ability to troubleshoot and support volunteers through their journey. Building this collaborative relationship with the fundraising team will not only enhance communications and coordination but also enable volunteers to contribute effectively and make a meaningful impact toward the fundraising goals.

If you are an executive leader leaning on volunteers to help with your fundraising, make sure you take time to build and support the team with clear expectations, goals, and a plan to implement those expectations and goals. Many

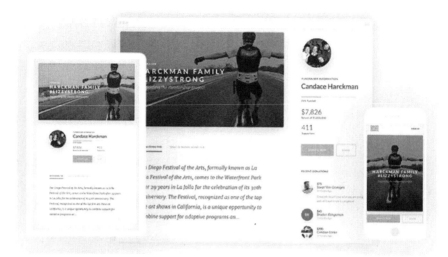

Peer-to-peer fundraising can be a fun way for volunteers to share their excitement for a new project at your organization.

Image courtesy of donately.com.

volunteers are excited to help in this capacity but quickly get discouraged if they are not able to see the forward momentum of donor relationships or gifts, or they feel undersupported without clear direction for their work. In the end, it is your responsibility to ensure that volunteers are prepared, excited, and engaged in any role they take on; and when they are not meeting expectations, they feel supported and understood.

Okay, enough words of caution—let's explore some ways volunteers have expressed interest and can support fundraising for museums small and large.

INTRODUCING VOLUNTEERS TO FUNDRAISING

For many small or volunteer-led museums, this is already a duty of volunteers. The board and volunteer staff of small organizations recognize the need for and importance of cultivating strategic relationships in order to generate income for operations costs (buildings, maintenance, office equipment, and supplies, etc.), developing new exhibitions and programs, creating outreach opportunities and special events, among other activities. Through fundraising opportunities like raffles, silent auctions, and community events, volunteers are already cultivating relationships with donors and asking for in-kind support via prizes and awards. In the case of raffles, bake sales, membership drives, or other peer-to-peer fundraising projects, volunteers are making a direct cash ask to museum donors in their community.

For small museums, these fundraising activities are a lifeline to not only maintain operations but to connect with the community and remind neighbors, family, friends, and other stakeholders what the museum has to offer. Volunteers are great ambassadors for the museum, and inviting them to participate in these peer-to-peer fundraising initiatives can, in many cases, help volunteers share their passion across a wider audience while engaging new faces in the museum experience through their personal network.

Peer-to-peer fundraising is often most successful when set up with a short timeline (like thirty days) or a certain goal in mind (think of those thermometer fundraisers or the cookie or candy sales of our youth). Having a limit to the fundraiser helps the volunteer express the urgency of giving to their network and generates anticipation and excitement around reaching a goal with friends. Membership drives and special project fundraising (do we all remember the crowdsourced campaign to save the spacesuit at a national museum?) are also great peer-to-peer fundraising opportunities for volunteers. Through this type of fundraising, they can share their personal connections, stories, and insights with the museum and its programs.

As a volunteer coordinator, you have an incredible opportunity to support your volunteers and the organization in raising the necessary funds to continue fulfilling the museum's mission. Volunteers can oftentimes get excited about sharing their stories during peer-to-peer fundraising campaigns, and that heart-to-heart story is essential to fundraising success. However, it is important for someone to maintain a central message around the campaign and ensure volunteers have the museum's mission, vision, and upcoming projects in mind whenever they are sharing news about the museum to donors and potential donors. This is not as scary as it sounds, but it is an important role to keep the messaging at the forefront and not get lost among personal stories from excited volunteers. A campaign manager or development colleague can help establish those important talking points and messages for the volunteers and help answer any questions that arise.

Ultimately through peer-to-peer fundraising, volunteers can help diversify the donor pipeline and allow nontraditional donors an entry point to the museum for giving and participation. By further cultivating the new donors, volunteers can help foster deeper relationships between community members and museum staff resulting in future giving and stewarding long-term relationships with more community members.

ENGAGING IN DONOR CULTIVATION AND STEWARDSHIP

It is a near-universal truth to say that volunteers may be some of the most passionate advocates and ambassadors a museum will ever have. Their commitment to the organization through their donation of time and expertise highlights how passionate most of our volunteers are for the mission they serve. This passion can be contagious, especially in donor circles when cash and other resource investments are at stake. But long before any big task is made, great development teams take time to cultivate relationships with donors, understand their donor's motivations for getting involved with an organization, and explore ways they (the donors) feel they can make an impact at the museum. A great tour, an engaging program, and a well-documented or organized collection area are all things that interest donors when they explore relationships with museums.

As we have discussed in previous chapters, these are some of the same projects volunteers work on day in and day out. In the case of small museums or departments, volunteers may be the only people working on some of these projects daily or weekly, making noticeable progress. Allowing volunteers to share their stories with donors and potential donors as they move through the development pipeline helps volunteers feel appreciated by the organization for their dedication of time and expertise to a project A donor will feel appreciation by connecting with a diverse group of museum stakeholders and seeing or hearing how their gifts have impacted the museum and community in a more personal way. This personal connection to the museum helps the development team cultivate a more appropriate and successful task for a donor as they continue to cultivate and steward their relationships.

Transitioning from cultivating relationships to making asks and securing gifts from volunteers is a delicate and crucial step. Once a strong foundation of trust and appreciation has been established, your development team can confidently approach volunteers to discuss potential contributions.

As the volunteer coordinator, you are the volunteer's advocate for all things in your museum. Even though the development team will be handling the ask, that does not mean that you should not be involved. Touch base with your volunteers to make sure they still feel valued and are being treated well by the other departments in the museum. Also, check that they are still excited by their expanding involvement in the museum. By recognizing the value and impact your volunteers bring to the organization, and leveraging their passion and expertise, museums can effectively solicit gifts from your dedicated volunteers.

MAKING ASKS AND SECURING GIFTS

This area of fundraising with volunteers tends to be the most controversial among fundraising staff and leadership. In organizations that have a robust and successful development department, it should absolutely be the responsibility of that staff to generally secure gifts, especially major gifts and gifts of assets and property to the organization, and volunteer donations are completely driven by the volunteers themselves. Because of legal ramifications for both the donor and the organization, it is important that whoever is involved in major giving activities is well versed in the legal nuances of charitable giving and maintaining relationships with donors to ensure a healthy and positive donor experience.

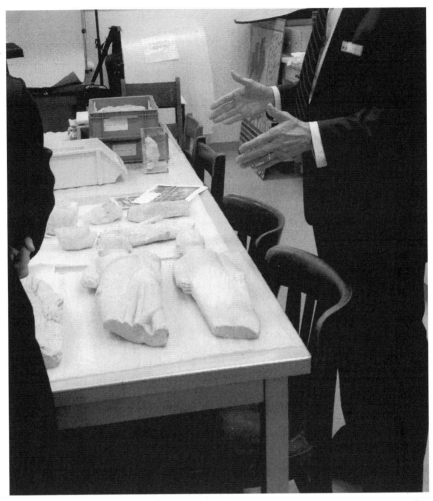

Volunteers can help advocate for all the treasures that lie within the museum vault.
Image courtesy of authors.

But we have found that many small museums, museums in remote locations or underserved communities, do not have that expertise on staff—if they even have staff, let alone staff dedicated solely to development. Here is where volunteers and volunteer boards step in to help make an organization sustainable by supporting growth among (and outside) the museum's community. As mentioned previously, it is important to have policies, procedures, and mechanisms in place to support, track, and report the types of gifts the organization is prepared to accept. This can be a major concern for fundraising professionals inviting volunteers into the ask phase of fundraising. We do not have the space in this publication to create a how-to for volunteers in fundraising, so this section serves as a catalyst to allow volunteer-run organizations to think about how they can be effective in fundraising, even without a professional development staff to fall back on.

There are a few types of tasks that volunteers can do to support the ongoing financial health of their museum. Volunteers, as explored previously, can create peer-to-peer fundraising opportunities to get friends involved and give to the museum the volunteer cares deeply about. If the museum holds a charitable status (usually a 501c3 in the United States, or registered charitable status in places like Canada or the United Kingdom), volunteers can assist in writing grants and grant reports or cultivating relations with local and national foundations that fund projects the museum is embarking on.

Museum volunteers may have networks that expand to local government officials that help open doors to government funding for capital projects or other special events or anniversaries. Museum volunteers may also have connections throughout the community that lend themselves to gift-in-kind tasks (such as building materials to construct new exhibits or program supplies from local shops). All these gifts should be part of the fundraising plan as donor recognition and stewardship plans are implemented upon the receipt of any gift secured either by volunteers or staff.

Volunteers love to share their experiences with their networks outside the organization.
Image courtesy of the authors.

Many museums also have volunteer boards that are seated because of their ability to connect with major stakeholders for fundraising or resource development. Boards tend to have their own handbook and operational plans and work closely with museum leadership to implement strategic plans. Volunteer coordinators generally are less involved with the direct relationship building and project management of the board, as museum leadership tends to supervise any strategic operations that need to come down to volunteers through volunteer coordinators, but it is worthwhile to provide updates and support leadership when needed to cultivate board relationships.

As a volunteer coordinator, your responsibility lies with ensuring that the volunteers who have expressed interest in getting involved in fundraising have the information they need to be successful in their activity. You also need to ensure that they can connect with the right museum representatives when it comes time to accept a gift. Moreover, you should foster opportunities where volunteers can get involved with donor stewardship and share their experiences with donors and community stakeholders. This will help to foster deeper relationships with the museum. With a bit of coordination, volunteers can support fundraising activities with the same vigor and success they support other activities across the museum and even help foster a more diverse and inclusive group of donors and stakeholders to help the museum support and grow with its community into the future.

NOTE

1. Eric Burger, "40 Volunteer Statistics That Will Blow Your Mind," VolunteerHub, November 9, 2021, https://volunteerhub.com/blog/40-volunteer-statistics.

7

Supporting Volunteer Boards and Volunteer Leadership

This chapter is dedicated to small museums, rural museums, grassroots organizations, and those operating with limited resources and staff. Often, these organizations heavily rely on volunteer boards and leadership to drive their mission forward. The relationship between the volunteer coordinator and the board is important for many reasons. From supporting inclusion opportunities for board members, enhancing governance and strategic development, to fostering a deeper appreciation for diversity and accessibility to achieve organizational success, being the liaison between the board and the rest of the museum volunteers is an exciting leadership role for any volunteer coordinator to step into.

By fostering collaboration across teams, maximizing board member engagement in the volunteer program, and providing support to the executive director or other museum leadership, the volunteer coordinator plays a crucial role in building and maintaining a successful volunteer board. This chapter explores strategies for nurturing a productive volunteer board in small museums, rural museums, grassroots organizations, and those with limited resources, empowering them to make a lasting impact.

Please note that throughout this chapter we will reference the top staff position as the *executive director*, but we would like to recognize that not all museums have this position and as such the term *executive director* serves as a catch-all title for the person(s) in charge of the day-to-day operations of the museum and is the one most likely to liaise with the board regularly. This position may also be staffed by a volunteer in some organizations, but we hope that the guiding principles presented throughout this chapter are helpful to the person filling this role.

BUILDING A SUCCESSFUL VOLUNTEER BOARD

As a volunteer coordinator, you play a vital role in supporting the executive director in building a successful volunteer board. While you may not directly manage the board, your expertise and insights can greatly assist in guiding and participating in the recruitment and retention processes. By understanding the importance of acknowledging and valuing the time commitments of board members, you can help create an environment that not only attracts dedicated individuals but fosters their growth and commitment to the organization for years to come.

A successful volunteer board should reflect the diversity of the organization's stakeholders, including current and potential audiences, community members, visitors, and other groups with which the museum hopes to engage. Taking the time to ensure that stakeholders are represented can help to make sure that decisions made by the board and leadership align with the museum's mission and resonate with its target audience and potential audiences. Finding individuals who not only represent the museum's stakeholders but champion the mission, vision, and work is crucial in supporting any board. A wide range of expertise among board members can greatly enhance decision making and bring fresh perspectives to the table.

Just like operational volunteers, strategic volunteers, such as board members, can be recruited through open calls or via personal networks. In the end, each person who wishes to serve on the board or in a strategic group needs to go through an application process to be vetted and interviewed to ensure they are a great fit for the organization. As the organization's volunteer coordinator, it is okay to offer your support and resources (applications, interview matrix,

Having a board that represents your community will inspire new stakeholders to get involved.

Image by pressfoto on Freepik.

and onboarding documents) to those responsible for recruiting and appointing board members and other strategic volunteers. Organizations that rely on their volunteer coordinator's resources for operational and strategic volunteers find their teams are more aligned after the onboarding process than those who leave the initial introduction to the organization to various department leaders or administrators.

Once a board member has joined the team, there are important steps a volunteer coordinator can take to support a successful and hardworking board. In your role, you can collaborate with the executive director to establish clear strategic goals that are achievable within the organization's capacity. By working closely with the executive director and sharing your insights on volunteer needs and expectations, you can help shape the roadmap that guides the efforts of the board and ensures alignment with the museum's long-term vision.

Maintaining open lines of communication between staff/operations and the board/strategic leadership is essential for a strong partnership and a sustainable organization. By actively participating in these discussions and providing updates on volunteer-related matters, you can foster a collaborative environment that encourages effective decision making, exceptional opportunities for development, and an engaging organization that represents all museum stakeholders. Your expertise in volunteer management can be instrumental in facilitating these conversations, ensuring that volunteer-related needs are appropriately addressed, troubleshooting policies are in place, and volunteer commitments and time are celebrated at all levels in the organization.

Your executive director ultimately works for the board of directors and serves at their pleasure. As a volunteer coordinator, you can contribute to the success of the board by providing support and guidance in recruitment and retention efforts. By leveraging your understanding of the organization's needs and the qualities required in prospective board members, you can assist in identifying and attracting individuals who possess the necessary expertise and dedication to drive meaningful progress.

Establishing clear strategic goals that are achievable within the organization's capacity is essential. Volunteers need a roadmap to guide their efforts effectively and ensure alignment with the museum's long-term vision. Maintaining open lines of communication between staff/operations and the board/strategic leadership is key. Regular updates, transparent discussions about needs and deliverables, and promoting a collaborative environment foster a strong partnership between the board and the organization's staff. Successful volunteer boards and leaders not only are willing to contribute their time but also possess the necessary expertise to tackle the museum's goals and tasks effectively. A combination of dedication, skills, and passion can drive meaningful progress.

Providing support to leadership by way of recruitment, onboarding, and project engagement ensures that the board feels a part of the volunteer team.
Image courtesy of the authors.

RESOURCES FOR BOARD MANAGEMENT AND LEADING SUCCESSFUL CHANGE

After providing a brief overview of the challenges museums may encounter with their boards, this section will explore various resources available to assist organizations in board management. It will highlight consultants, programs, and best practices that can support small and grassroots museums in developing effective board governance and leading successful change through their boards. Nurturing volunteer boards and leadership in small and grassroots organizations is vital for their success. By following the principles outlined in this chapter, and utilizing available resources, these museums can build strong and effective boards that drive their missions forward.

It should be a priority for you to be prepared to support your museum's board and executive director, even if you may not work directly with board members. Each museum and executive director has unique policies and preferences regarding staff interactions with board members. However, knowing board management and dynamics can greatly benefit your role and enable you to provide valuable support when needed. While your primary focus may be on volunteer management, understanding that board members are volunteers and understanding the challenges that museums encounter with their boards is crucial. This knowledge allows you to appreciate the significance of nurturing volunteer boards and leadership in museums of all sizes, but especially in small and grassroots organizations.

By recognizing a volunteer board's importance, you can contribute to creating an environment that fosters collaboration and success. In some cases, volunteer coordinators may have direct interactions with board members, assisting in facilitating their involvement in volunteer programs or events. If this is the case for you, it becomes even more important to understand the principles of effective board governance and how to navigate the complexities of leading change through the boards. To support your museum's board and executive director effectively, it is beneficial to familiarize yourself with available resources and best practices.

While your involvement may differ from other staff members, having a basic understanding of board governance can help you align your efforts with the overall mission and goals of the organization. Although you may not be directly responsible for board management, you can still contribute to the museum's success by being aware of the resources and books that are available on the topic. This knowledge can assist you in providing informed recommendations or suggestions when appropriate, even if your involvement is limited to volunteer coordination. Consider exploring the following resources to expand your understanding of board governance and structure:

- Boards on Fire by Susan Howlett (2019), https://susanhowlett.com/boards-on-fire/
- "Managing Your Volunteer Board: 3 Ways to Deepen Engagement" by Jeb Banner (updated November 2, 2022), https://www.galaxydigital.com/blog/managing-your-volunteer-board-3-ways-to-deepen-engagement
- Nonprofit Financial Oversight: The Concise and Complete Guide for Boards and Finance Committees by Michael E. Batts, CPA (Scotts Valley, CA: CreateSpace Independent Publishing Platform), 2017.
- Onboarding Champions: The Seven Recruiting Principles of Highly Effective Nonprofit Boards by James Mueller (Delray Beach, FL: James Mueller & Assoc.), 2021.
- "Principles for Good Governance and Ethical Practice," Independent Sector, https://independentsector.org/sector-health/principles-for-good-governance/.
- The Little Book of Boards: A Board Member's Handbook for Small (and Very Small) Nonprofits by Erik Hanberg (Tacoma, WA: Side x Side Publishing), 2014.

- *The Nonprofit Board Answer Book: A Practical Guide for Board Members and Chief Executives*, third edition (San Francisco, CA: Jossey-Bass/Board-Source), 2012.
- "Running a Nonprofit" (find tools and resources on boards and good governance), National Council of Nonprofits, https://www.councilofnonprofits.org/running-nonprofit.
- "What Board Members Need to Know about Not-for-Profit Finance and Accounting," Jacobson Jarvis & Co., https://jjco.com/what-board-members-need-to-know-about-not-for-profit-finance-and-accounting/.
- "What Are the Board's Responsibilities for Volunteers?" by Susan J. Ellis, Blue Avocado, May 13, 2009, https://blueavocado.org/board-of-directors/what-are-the-board-s-responsibilities-for-volunteers/.

Additional blogs to follow for advice in supporting boards:

- *Ten Basic Responsibilities of Nonprofit Boards* (summary), BoardSource, https://boardsource.org/product/ten-basic-responsibilities-nonprofit-boards/
- Nonprofit Leadership Lab, https://nonprofitleadershiplab.com
- The Chronicle of Philanthropy, https://www.philanthropy.com
- Candid, https://blog.candid.org

By familiarizing yourself with these resources (and others through a quick web search for "managing museum boards" or "volunteer/nonprofit boards"), you can gain valuable insights and knowledge that will help you support the board and executive director in accordance with expectations. Your understanding of board management will enable you to provide the necessary guidance and assistance to volunteers who may interact with board members directly. While your primary role may be volunteer coordination, being prepared to support the board and executive director demonstrates your commitment to the overall success of the museum. By staying informed and understanding the policies and preferences regarding staff interactions with board members, you can contribute to a harmonious and effective working relationship that ultimately benefits the museum and its mission.

RETHINKING THE ROLE OF BOARDS AND STAFF

Let's rethink the roles of board members and staff members together. We have often been told that there should be a clear separation between the board's governance responsibilities as board members and the management responsibilities of the staff. However, there is now a debate emerging about whether this traditional division is still effective. This division was initially instituted across many organizations to prevent micromanagement day to day and prioritize long-term strategic planning; it may have unintentionally created a disconnect between board members and the day-to-day operations of the museums they serve. Perhaps it is time to reassess this divide and explore more integrated approaches that allow board members to have a deeper understanding of how our organizations work.

In smaller organizations, where resources are limited, board members often engage in hands-on work. As the museum grows and hires staff, these direct service activities are typically delegated, and the board's focus shifts more toward fundraising and long-range strategic planning. Paradoxically, the more removed the board is from day-to-day operations, the more prestigious and exclusive serving on the board becomes, and a strong relationship between staff leadership and the board becomes more crucial. This raises questions about the effectiveness of decision making when board members lack firsthand experience of the organization's work.

A strong board should consist of diverse members of the community with a variety of backgrounds, including those who may not be familiar with the organization's daily operations. However, all board members must have a basic understanding of the organization to govern effectively. Without this understanding, it becomes challenging to make informed decisions, advocate for support and funding, or evaluate the performance of the executive director.

To bridge this gap, it might be wise to ask volunteer board members to commit to spending a minimum number of hours a year at your museum supporting programming or connecting with back-of-house volunteers. Many boards encourage one to two hours per month (or around twelve hours a year) to spend time getting to know and observe what the museum does and how their work supports and sustains the day-to-day activities. This could involve observing operations, completing direct-service volunteer tasks, or shadowing staff members. Board members should recognize the limitations of making strategic decisions in the absence of firsthand data. It is important for us to address any prevailing sentiment among some paid executives who prefer board members to solely focus on fundraising and avoid involvement in operational matters. The board brings valuable expertise from different perspectives, which should not be discounted solely because it is not field-specific.

THE RELATIONSHIP BETWEEN THE BOARD AND THE VOLUNTEER COORDINATOR

The dynamics between the board and the volunteer coordinator can vary from one museum to another. The executive director often sets the tone and cadence of this relationship. Some executive directors prefer to be the sole point of contact for board members, limiting the involvement of the volunteer coordinator. However, it is crucial to consider the responsibilities of the volunteer coordinator, as you are responsible for managing and coordinating all volunteers, including board members who may also serve as volunteers.

Regardless of the level of involvement allowed by the executive director, the volunteer coordinator can still play a valuable role in supporting board members. One way to do this is by helping to create a meaningful onboarding process for new board members and participating in recognizing and valuing the time commitments of board members and the board as a whole. The welcoming and onboarding process can involve providing each board member with comprehensive information about the museum, its mission, programs, and volunteer opportunities. Some museums use their volunteer onboarding book and just add a section regarding board activities and responsibilities. The volunteer coordinator can also facilitate introductions to key staff members and provide resources that help board members understand their roles and responsibilities. After you have initially connected with board members, you can work with the museum leadership to continue your relationship through arranging ongoing training opportunities and facilitate recognition for service, special projects, or other important milestones your board celebrates.

In organizations where the volunteer coordinator is encouraged to have a more hands-on role with board members, they can actively work toward building a collaborative relationship. This can involve regular communication and updates on volunteer activities, volunteer needs, and opportunities for board members to engage directly with volunteers. By fostering this collaborative relationship, the volunteer coordinator can help board members gain a deeper

Celebrate your volunteers and their accomplishments as much as you can.
Image by Freepik.

understanding of the museum's volunteer program and the impact it has on achieving the organization's mission.

The volunteer coordinator can also play a crucial role in maximizing board member engagement by identifying volunteer opportunities that align with their skills, interests, and availability. This can include special projects, committee involvement, or even hands-on volunteer work that allows board members to experience the organization's mission firsthand. By actively involving board members in the volunteer program, the volunteer coordinator can help bridge the gap between the board and the organization's day-to-day operations.

Effective communication and collaboration between the volunteer coordinator, executive director, and board members are essential for a successful relationship. The executive director should clearly define the roles and expectations for the volunteer coordinator in supporting board members, while also ensuring that the volunteer coordinator has the necessary resources and authority to fulfill those responsibilities. Regular meetings and open lines of communication can facilitate a collaborative approach that benefits both the board and the volunteer program.

While the relationship between the volunteer coordinator and the board may vary based on the preferences of the executive director, it is important to recognize the potential value that the volunteer coordinator brings to supporting board members. By creating a meaningful onboarding process, fostering collaboration, and maximizing board member engagement in the volunteer program, the volunteer coordinator can contribute to a stronger and more connected governance structure. This collaborative relationship can enhance the effectiveness of the board in fulfilling the organization's mission and drive overall success.

While you may not directly manage the board, your role is crucial in supporting the executive director and contributing to the recruitment and retention of board members. By leveraging your expertise in volunteer management, providing input on strategic goals, and maintaining open lines of communication, you can help build a successful volunteer board that aligns with the museum's mission and drives meaningful progress.

Part III

Putting It All Together: Volunteerism Today

8

Museum Volunteerism in Action

HYPOTHETICAL CASES

The following hypothetical situations have been created to help you imagine how the principles explored in the previous chapters can be put into practice in everyday scenarios. These fictional case studies are based on real-life experiences shared by our colleagues and volunteers. Additionally, our daily interactions with dedicated teams have further inspired these narratives. We strive to represent a diversity of museums and volunteers but know there is no way we can capture all the scenarios you may encounter in your tenure as a volunteer coordinator. We hope you will find inspiration in the scenarios we have created, and that they lead you to connect what you have learned in previous chapters of this book with your own experiences to help you overcome challenges you may face in your role so that you can celebrate wonderful successes with your team, over and over again.

The scenarios will examine different museums as well as different types of volunteers. Each scene will begin with a mini dossier on the subject. It will include the name of the subject, as well as their occupation, hobbies, and the specific type of museum in which they chose to volunteer. These scenarios are fictional but were designed to help volunteer coordinators find the connection between the principles in the previous chapters and real-life applications. The end of each case study will highlight the main lessons and pose questions to consider about your program in relation to the scenario presented, as well as accessibility considerations that should be in the volunteer coordinator's forethought when creating a volunteer experience similar to the case presented. The lessons, questions, and considerations are intended to spark a discussion among your team members and better prepare you for creating and maintaining a volunteer program.

Please do not hesitate to reference this chapter as often as necessary to work through scenarios you face in your role, use some of the scenarios presented in your training and handbooks, or engage your organizational leadership in a volunteer management exercise. By exploring principles in action, it is easier to get the whole team thinking and discussing how they would participate in a similar scenario at your museum. We hope these become conversation starters for you and your team as often as you need.

THE EVENT VOLUNTEER

Name: Julie (she/her)
   Occupation: Technology entrepreneur
   Hobbies: Reading novels, hiking, and traveling to visit family and friends
   Museum: Local County Museum

Julie has spent her professional life working to create a new technology used in the medical field. She studied extensively at a nationally ranked tech school and with some classmates decided to take their capstone project to market. The team has spent the last ten years testing their technology and seeking necessary patents and clearances to take their device to the open market. After lots of hard work and long hours dedicated to the project, the team formed a company and launched the technology to the public—with rave reviews. Julie is ecstatic to have pushed her dream to reality, but now she is looking for a project that allows her to reconnect with her community and have new social experiences. Julie's friend suggested she reach out to the local museum to see if they had any volunteer openings for their upcoming season.

Julie was thrilled by the idea that she could give back to her community and emailed the museum to learn more about opportunities for involvement at the museum. Julie headed off to the office to start her busy day of meetings and investor reporting. The day ended and Julie drove home, past the county museum. She noticed a flier in the window for an upcoming program, and for the rest of the drive home, she dreamed about helping with the program. One day turned into another day and then a third. Julie was starting to wonder if the museum got her message. Knowing how busy life gets, she decided to wait until the weekend to stop by and follow up.

Over lunch, Julie got a chance to check her phone and saw that a message had come in during her last meeting. The voicemail suggested Julie give the museum a call back during business hours to further discuss opportunities to volunteer. Although she was excited to connect with the volunteer coordinator, Julie knew she was not going to be able to break away the rest of the week and chat during business hours. Still, Julie decided that she would send an email to the general email address again asking that her message be forwarded to the volunteer coordinator, Saryah.

Subject: Volunteer inquiry follow-up Attn: Saryah

Hi Saryah,

Thank you for the call today, I am sorry I missed it. I am very excited to connect with you and chat about some opportunities for me to volunteer at the museum. Unfortunately, my work schedule for the next few weeks will not allow me to break free during the day. I wanted to connect with you directly via email so that we can continue the conversation asynchronously. I am interested in helping with the upcoming event and I hope that there might be an opportunity for me to do so. Is there a form or information you need from me to get the volunteer process started?

Warm wishes,

Julie

Saryah followed up the next afternoon with an email thanking Julie for reaching out and apologizing for the call. They were happy to reach out through email and Saryah invited Julie to the museum for a quick face-to-face meeting over the weekend. Julie was delighted by the reply, and they set a time to meet on Saturday afternoon.

Julie and Saryah met at the admission table and took a quick tour through the galleries. They then headed to Saryah's office where Julie was given an official application form. While filling it out, Saryah shared some of the opportunities available at the museum for volunteers that season. Julie noted her professional experience on her application as well as her passion for reading novels and being outdoors. Saryah noticed Julie had an amazing skill set and knew that the archivist was desperately looking for help organizing a digitization project. She shared that opportunity with Julie.

Julie listened patiently but was not interested in another technology project. She had been working so hard that she is now interested in making friends and learning something new. Julie mentioned to Saryah that she preferred to do a project outside of her professional experience and referenced the poster she saw in the window for the upcoming open house program. Julie mentioned she loves spending time outdoors and would be more than happy to help with logistics for the day of the event.

Disappointed that they could not convince Julie to jump into the digital archives project, Saryah recognized the hint and turned the discussion to the upcoming event. The museum was hosting a special training for the event in two weeks, on a Thursday at 5 p.m. Saryah asked Julie if she would be able to make the training session, noting that Julie was usually in the office during business hours. They also mentioned that there was a general volunteer training session next Monday night and that all volunteers are encouraged to attend a training session to help orient them to the organization and meet other new volunteers. Julie was on board for both evenings and shared with Saryah that she is very excited to get started.

Not wanting to curb Julie's enthusiasm for volunteering, Saryah pulled a small binder off the shelf and handed it to Julie. They explained that this was a binder full of material that all volunteers get when they start. Julie should take some time before Monday to look through the material and bring it to the evening sessions. She took the material, and Saryah walked Julie out to the galleries. Julie wandered a bit more and headed home excited to review the material she had received at the museum.

Monday was a long day at work and Julie was exhausted but knew that Saryah had booked her for the first training session for that night. Julie grabbed some takeout and headed to the museum for the evening. To her delight, a friend from high school was sitting in the room finishing his takeout too! Julie headed over and joined Mike where they spent some time catching up while other new volunteers came into the room and started chatting. Saryah also joined the group and quickly made the rounds to welcome each volunteer and thank them for coming out for the evening.

They kicked off the training session, quickly going over the mission and programs of the museum along with the staff chart. This quick orientation helped all the volunteers settle in and begin to think about the museum and how they could contribute to the museum's mission through their work. Saryah then went around the room and asked each person to introduce themselves. Among the group there was Julie, along with two other working professionals, two college interns, one high school volunteer, and a group of five retired neighbors who volunteer with a new organization every year as a group (#retirementgoals, Julie thought to herself!).

Saryah took some time to go over several opportunities at the museum and then covered some general history of the area, frequently asked questions and situations volunteers face while at the museum, and some of the emergency procedures for when there is severe weather, which is more than likely at their site. Finally, the floor was opened for discussion and questions. The rest of the evening was an exhilarating mix of questions about logistics, trivia about the museum and its collection, and general discussion among the volunteers. Julie was energized and inspired by the time she got in her car for the drive home.

The second training was just as exhilarating, and Julie decided she was comfortable joining the team for the upcoming open house. Julie reached out to Saryah to check in. Saryah was delighted to hear from Julie and confirmed that they need Julie to help with wayfinding from the back parking lot to the museum's front door. Knowing that this will be Juile's first time working, Saryah sent Julie all the information she would need for the day and connected her to a seasoned volunteer. This volunteer would be working with Julie on the day of the event.

Saryah hoped that Julie was comfortable with the job and all the information she had received. Saryah knew that if a volunteer had a great first experience, they would keep coming back for more events, eventually transitioning to regular shifts. Saryah had a hunch that Julie might be interested in more projects and events once she finds her footing at the museum, and they were excited to support Julie's journey each step of the way.

LESSONS

- Make volunteer opportunities easy to find on your website and share on social media. Peer-to-peer recommendations always carry the most weight, so the more people who know you are in need of volunteers, the more likely you will find a great fit.
- Have flexibility in your schedule to meet with a new volunteer. Creating a rigid schedule and single modes of communication not only eliminates some potential volunteers, but the lack of accommodation for schedules, communication preferences, and other needs of a new or seasoned volunteer may leave the volunteer feeling discouraged and unwilling to pursue the opportunity further.
- Provide opportunities for volunteers to connect with each other and museum staff throughout their shifts and beyond. The more you nurture the community-building in your volunteer team, the more committed and supportive the team will be for the museum.
- Remember to continue to foster your volunteer's growth and development on the team. A great experience leads a volunteer to inquire about more opportunities. By fostering that excitement, a one-time volunteer can quickly turn into a regular.

QUESTIONS TO PONDER

1. Are you able to create opportunities for working professionals to volunteer at your organization?
2. Are you able to provide flexible training, onboarding, and working shifts for professionals or busy adults?
3. Work with your development team to build a *corporate social responsibility* program that allows companies the opportunity to volunteer at an event or on a project as a team, and usually serves as one component of a larger sponsorship for the organization.

ACCESSIBILITY CONSIDERATIONS

- For event and program-based volunteers, it is important to make sure that they are comfortable moving around the environment in which they are working. If a volunteer has mobility devices, are the areas in which they work accommodating to their device?

- Make sure that volunteers who are delivering instructions to visitors and participants can communicate clearly and easily. If a volunteer is not a native language speaker for your area, make sure they are comfortable enough to communicate with patrons if questions come up. Perhaps some extra training on local slang might be helpful to a newcomer volunteering at your organization. Additionally, if a volunteer relies on a communication device or tool, it is a good idea to make sure they are comfortable in their role using that device. In some cases, voice recognition may work in a quiet room or one-on-one conversation, but in a large and noisy festival, it may struggle with background noise. Is there a solution that works best for the volunteers, the visitors, and the museum?
- Events can be very busy, noisy, and exciting. It is a good idea to check with each volunteer on their tolerance level for sensory overload. Make sure to plan a break schedule and offer a quiet place to decompress for all your volunteers during their breaks, including refreshments and comfortable places to sit down and recharge. If a volunteer expresses they are at their maximum capacity for their senses, take the opportunity to support their needs and allow them time away from the event to recharge or head home. Respecting your volunteers' needs will go a long way in having them feel supported by the organization and endear them to the museum for future volunteer opportunities.

THE COLLECTION VOLUNTEER

Name: Jamal (he/him)
   Occupation: University student
   Hobbies: Drawing, hiking, listening to trivia podcasts
   Museum: Regional County Museum

Jamal is a graduate student studying geology at the local university. He has been fascinated by fossils and rocks since he was young. As one of the first kids in his family to graduate from high school, Jamal continued his studies, not only through an undergraduate degree but he also received a scholarship to study geology with a promise of a position with a top company upon completion of his degrees. Because of this, Jamal has been super focused on achieving the marks he needs to successfully graduate and land a great job.

Throughout his academic journey, Jamal has kept in touch with a mentor who helped him through his first semester in college. He took a paleontology class for fun, and his professor had many discussions with him about how archaeologists and paleontologists contribute to big business, city operations, and sustainability planning through roles beyond the fieldwork most of the public sees. The idea of having a job that supports his community while doing something he loves has fueled Jamal's commitment to his studies.

As Jamal was finishing his last term, his mentor suggested he look into an opportunity to get some volunteer hours on his résumé. The company Jamal is planning to work for upon graduation encourages their employees to spend time working in their community. This helps their employees really understand the needs the community faces and learn more about the resources and opportunities the company can create to support those needs both locally and globally.

Jamal settles on trying to find a place that allows him to put some of his education to work for him right away and finds a flier on a community board at the local coffee shop where he spends time studying. The flier is for the regional museum that is looking for volunteers to help them prepare for a new exhibit at the museum. They need volunteers who are comfortable working independently on research projects, recordkeeping, writing, and construction.

On the flier is a phone number and email for the volunteer coordinator at the museum, as well as some pictures of volunteers hard at work in the back rooms of the museum! Jamal had never thought of volunteering for a museum, in fact, he had nearly skimmed past the flier until he noticed a rare fossil in a drawer in one of the pictures. Jamal had only read about them in class, so to see that the local museum had one in their collection caught Jamal's attention right away.

While waiting for his coffee, Jamal quickly drafted an email to the volunteer coordinator introducing himself, sharing his academic background, and his hopes to work at the museum during his last term at school. He mentioned his particular interest in fossils and geology and asked to be considered for any work that may allow him the chance to view the fossil and rock collection at the museum.

A few days later Jamal received a reply from the volunteer office at the museum. They would be delighted to have a geology expert come into the museum and help them process their collection. As it just so happens, part of the next exhibit involves exploring the local natural resources and how they have shaped the community. The email also included a volunteer application and a request for references. When Jamal got home, he took time to fill out the application and send notes to his references regarding his application to the museum. He then replied to the museum with his availability for a meeting, his application and references, and how the project aligned perfectly with his anticipated role after graduation.

By the end of the month, Jamal had been interviewed by the volunteer coordinator, Tim. He was welcomed to the team and connected with a seasoned volunteer, Judy. He began learning about the museum, its exhibitions, and its collections. Judy worked with the archivist during her regular shifts at the museum. She had been a librarian during her working life. In retirement, Judy decided she missed the library, but really wanted to explore hidden stories about her community and started volunteering at the museum to help process the backlog of archival material. She mentioned to Jamal that he was going to be tasked to do the same thing. The backlog of natural history collections had been causing the curator some sleepless nights, and with the new mission to highlight more collection items in relation to current community successes and challenges, the whole back-of-house team was stressed trying to get more collections ready for exhibition and publication. Once Jamal had a sense of the mission, Judy was ready to take him to the curatorial department and help him learn about processing objects.

After a couple of shifts taking tours of the galleries and sitting in on programs, Jamal felt like he was ready to explore the back-of-house, specifically the fossils! He was so excited to get his first look at the drawers of specimens and explore the history of natural resources in his area. On the appointed day, Jamal arrived at the museum to meet Judy for the collection rooms walk-through. They spent two hours exploring the library, the archive stacks, the history collections, a special room for intake and pest control, and then finally, on the other side of the space were the natural collections. The collections consisted of various types of local flora and fauna, skillfully preserved using a diverse range of materials. Among them were medical collections, including outdated technology, as well as a big area marked *ROCKS*. Jamal giggled, obviously a nongeologist labeled that aisle. He could not wait to open the drawers and see what was really inside!

As Judy and Jamal looked through the drawers, Jamal shared what each specimen was and why it was important. Judy stood back and listened to all the information Jamal had to share. She knew that he was exactly what the museum needed to get these collections in order and ready to use. As they were peeking in the last drawer, Nate, the curator at the museum, came in to introduce themself and apologize for missing Jamal's first walk-through as they were on vacation but had heard about Jamal's background and did not want to waste any time getting Jamal into the volunteer corps.

Nate, Judy, and Jamal then went to the break room to chat about the project and get Jamal trained on the collection database and cataloging systems. Judy was familiar with the archival process but did not know the object collection process very well. Nate assured them both that to start, a few exercises Judy and Jamal could do together would be great. Then Nate and Jamal could plan another time to work in the geology collections specifically.

By the end of the museum visit, Judy, Jamal, and Nate had a plan for the next visit and a timeline for starting the collection project. Jamal was able to get time cleared in his school schedule for a mock internship. He did not need the credits, but the classification allowed him to spend some class time working at the museum instead of another extra course to maintain his full-time registration at the university.

Over the next term, Jamal came to the museum every week to spend an afternoon with the collections. After the first couple of weeks with Nate, Jamal was comfortable handling the specimens, noting their size, shape, and chemical makeup as far as he could tell visually, as well as noting other interesting facts in the digital catalog record (such as the likely or known location of discovery, historical use for the resource, known other samples in museum collections around the world, and interesting uses for exhibitions or programs).

Jamal made notes on changes in technology and how the geologic resources were being used now by the local community and nationally. As he found exceptional pieces, Jamal called Nate and then discussed how they could use the pieces in the new exhibit Nate was working on. By the time Jamal's term ended, Nate and Jamal had come up with the prime pieces for the new exhibition and a nearly completed update to the inventory in the geology collections.

Jamal was disappointed he was not able to get into the fossil collection, but he knew the work he had done made a big impact on the museum. He had a new mentor and expanded his network by working with Nate and was excited to come back and see how the specimens he chose for the exhibit would come together in the gallery. Jamal was sad to walk out of the museum after his last shift, but a job well done meant his heart was filled and he knew he would be checking back regularly.

A few days later Jamal met with his new employer. They were already impressed with Jamal's commitment to his academics and had offered to hold a position for him if he was dedicated to finishing his graduate degree. Jamal shared that one of his most memorable experiences during his schooling was actually the volunteer work he did at the museum. He was able to put his studies to work and help an organization prepare to celebrate the natural world around them. He detailed how he worked with teams across the museum and worked directly with the curator Nate to develop part of an upcoming exhibit.

Jamal's employer was so impressed with the work Jamal completed while in school, they asked if it was possible for Jamal to connect the marketing team with Nate. The company did not know the museum was planning to develop an exhibit celebrating local natural resources, and they wanted to explore ways to be involved in the project. Jamal thought it would be a great opportunity and connected with Nate as soon as he got to his desk.

LESSONS

- Subject-matter experts make excellent collection and back-of-house volunteers as their knowledge may help fill gaps in the catalog record or exhibition story. Be sure to learn what your volunteer's interests are and try to match those interests with volunteer experience. Remember to listen to their feedback and if they want a new or different challenge, work with them to make the most out of their volunteer experience.
- Students are often looking for ways to earn credit hours while gaining professional experience, or, in some cases, volunteer hours or internships

are required for graduation. Take time to consider partnerships with local schools and universities. Having strong working partnerships with schools allows students to gain access to on-the-job skills training at your organization while the school can prepare the student volunteers for what to expect during their time working at the museum. The stronger the partnership, the more prepared students, their supervisors, and your staff can and will be for supporting student volunteers and interns.

Volunteers, no matter what stage of their careers, can become huge advocates for the museum among their professional and personal networks. Supporting volunteers and engaging them in both the successes and the challenges (within reason) of the organization can help them become passionate advocates for the museum by seeking support from the community through their networks.

QUESTIONS TO PONDER

1. Are you able to structure a volunteer experience to match the curriculum needs of local high schools or post-secondary schools?
2. Does your development or fundraising team reach out to businesses to discuss volunteer opportunities and matching grants for employee community service?
3. Do your volunteer marketing materials show the type of activities volunteers do at your organization, or does the material highlight collection items or special exhibits the volunteers get to work with?
4. How can you highlight something that makes volunteering with you a unique experience?
5. Do other departments depend on the volunteer office to recruit and train their volunteers in addition to general operations volunteers?

ACCESSIBILITY CONSIDERATIONS

• When working with museum collections, it is important to ensure the physical safety of the volunteer, the objects the volunteer is handling, and the rest of the objects and storage mechanisms the volunteer may need to navigate around. Having equipment to help the volunteer move and manipulate objects for cataloging is important, as well as establishing clear workplace safety guidelines. Volunteers, like staff, should be trained in all the guidelines set forth by the museum, and assistance can be offered to volunteers where it is safe. But, if a project requires lifting, moving in potentially hazardous ways, or requiring personal protective equipment, it is important that those requirements are disclosed to any volunteer early, and that the correct equipment is provided for and easily accessible to the volunteer. If moving, lifting, or handling any collection item, especially hazardous material, is hard or uncomfortable for a volunteer, the staff needs to be responsive and support the volunteer as necessary.

- In addition, other physical considerations need to be made for volunteers who may use mobility devices or have sensitivities to light, sound, or temperature. Take a moment to evaluate the physical spaces volunteers need to move through and work in while they are serving as back-of-house collection volunteers. Do the stacks provide enough space for a wheelchair to navigate? Are the lights too dim for someone who may be faced with visual challenges? Is the storage room at a comfortable temperature to spend long periods of time in, or are there ways to move artifacts to a comfortable workstation for the project and return them to storage after each shift? Are there ambient noises or lights that may be distracting or upsetting to some volunteers? Evaluating the environment for triggers and stressors, as well as taking time to understand alternative ways of moving in the space, will help you prepare your collection volunteers to be their best selves while working with the museum's collections.

THE VISITOR-FACING VOLUNTEER

Name: Dana (he/him)
> *Occupation*: Retired corporate accounts manager
> *Hobbies*: Cooking, traveling, and recently Dana has taken up boatbuilding with friends
> *Museum*: Science and Technology Museum

When Dana and his partner were looking for a place to settle for retirement, they had their pick of choices. Should they head to the mountains? Should they head to the beach? Should they head to where their daughter was setting up her own home and family nowhere near the mountains or the beach? Dana had dreamed of retiring to a nice beachside cottage or a cottage near some of the best skiing they could find, while his partner dreamed of a house full of grandchildren and family dinners every week.

Dana loved being a dad and was eagerly awaiting the newest addition to the family. Granddad was a bonus role Dana was excited to take on, so together they decided that it is easy to head to the beach or the mountains when they want, but missing milestones with their daughter and her new family was something neither of them wanted. So their retirement location was decided and Dana's new home has a lot of outdoor activities including areas to hike, lakes to boat around, and lots of great new food places to explore. Settling in was going well, but with the change in weather, Dana was looking for some opportunities to get out of the house but not necessarily outside during the cold season.

As they were watching the morning news, Dana's partner drew his attention to an event happening at the science and technology museum downtown. They were having a guest speaker who was presenting a series of lectures on the growing use of artificial intelligence and how early computers set the stage for the evolution into virtual reality and artificial intelligence. The news mentioned there would be a number of opportunities to meet the speaker throughout the week and the museum welcomed anyone to RSVP for lectures and events. While running errands later that day Dana popped by the museum to find out more about the special lecture series. Before he left the museum he had signed up for the first lecture.

The night came and Dana and his partner had a nice meal and then ventured to the museum for the special lecture. While they were waiting for the doors of the auditorium to open for the event, Dana and his partner walked around and looked at the pop-up displays. As they were looking at a display on changes in calculator technology, a museum volunteer came over to answer questions and share some interesting tidbits about the artifacts in the case. Throughout their conversation other visitors stopped to look at the display, and the volunteer would welcome them and ask if they had questions while continuing the conversation with Dana and his partner.

After a few minutes, there was a small crowd swapping stories about bringing new technology into the workplace and swapping funny stories of troubleshooting a fax machine or getting the first office computers hooked up to the internet, and reflecting on how business changed after each big advance in technology. Dana was excited to find others he could talk business with. He did not miss going to work but discovered he missed swapping stories and memories with others who had worked in similar industries throughout their careers.

The lecture was great, and some more technology win-and-fail stories were shared throughout the evening. Dana was struck by the questions and stories that were being shared and wondered if there were tickets left for the rest of the series. At the end of the evening, there was a reception where the stories continued. Dana found the museum representative who checked them in for the evening and asked if additional tickets were available. The museum representative had the unfortunate job of telling Dana that they were sold out for the rest of the series.

Disappointed, Dana said thank you for the information, and as he turned, the museum representative asked if he had any experience with serving as an usher at events, as they were short a couple of volunteers to help make sure attendees were checked in and could find a seat in the auditorium when the doors opened. Dana wanted to learn more. The museum representative asked Dana to leave his email and phone number and told him the volunteer coordinator would reach out in the morning to chat more about what shifts needed to be filled for the upcoming lectures. Thanking her for her time and leaving his contact info for the volunteer coordinator, Dana and his partner headed home, reflecting on their night at the museum.

Amanda, the volunteer coordinator, called Dana the next morning. They chatted about the previous night's program, the pop-up exhibits, and how struck Dana was by the group that formed at the display and enjoyed sharing personal stories about their workplace technology. Amanda was glad to hear Dana had such a great night and that Dana was interested in attending the rest of the lectures in the series. Dana did want to attend additional lectures but had been told that the tickets were sold out but that there might be an opportunity to volunteer at some of the lectures.

Amanda walked through the schedule and the shifts she needed to be filled. She had a couple of usher positions for two lectures and needed help at the check-in table for another lecture. She took time to explain each of the job requirements to Dana and asked if he had any interest and experience in volunteering. She told him he would be able to sneak into the back of the lecture once it started and listen in, but that he would likely have to stand, and may be interrupted if someone needed assistance getting to or from their seat while the lecture was on.

Dana thought this was great. He was okay with the physical requirements and was happy to help people to or from their spots while getting to listen in on the additional expert lectures. Amanda was delighted and told Dana that she would have a polo shirt for him to wear on his first shift and that he should come dressed according to the dress code for volunteers at the museum. Not a problem—Dana had all he needed in his closet. They went through a few more logistics and information that Dana may need each night to help answer general questions about the museum. When they were done, Dana and Amanda agreed to have a chat the morning after Dana's first shift to check in and answer any additional questions.

On the appointed day, Dana got ready early and headed to the museum. Amanda had suggested that if he had some time before his next shift, he should come early and have a walk around a gallery or two. One of the perks of being a museum volunteer was free admission, and she would leave his new volunteer name badge at the front if he thought he might come in early. Dana had a late lunch with his family and headed off to the museum. He had never walked through the science and technology museum before and wanted to take advantage of the opportunity.

As he turned the corner in a gallery dedicated to weather forecasting, he overheard a facilitator talking about how tornadoes are tracked by Doppler radar and by storm chasers who follow radar and try to collect data to improve predictions and weather patterns. Dana was fascinated by the interaction of technology and on-the-ground scientific observation. He found himself perching on a nearby bench to hear the rest of the discussion. The school children were on the edges of their seats too and asked really great questions that led to some in-depth discussion about weather safety at home.

The breadth of the conversation amazed Dana, and when the group moved on, he took another couple minutes to soak in all the information he had heard. The rest of the afternoon in the gallery was educational and Dana had fun observing visitors and how they were interacting with the exhibits. He even helped a couple of young kids turn a big crank to move a cloud across a diorama to mimic how temperatures change in the shade.

Already having spent what felt like a full day at the museum, Dana headed to the auditorium to check in with Amanda, collect his new shirt, and get a quick orientation for the evening. As other volunteers gathered, Dana introduced himself and chatted about the museum, families, and plans for the winter. Amanda joined the group of ushers, pop-up facilitators, and check-in volunteers. She ran down the schedule for the evening, pointed out the easiest and most accessible paths to the restrooms and water fountains; where the emergency phone was; and how to contact the security guards on duty should there be an emergency. Dana was set to get to work and joined his fellow ushering team at the doors to the auditorium.

The evening went off without a hitch, and Dana even got to sit through most of the lecture and discussion. He was delighted that he was able to provide some assistance to an older couple who had ventured in to learn about a topic their grandson was studying in school, and now they could have a conversation with him, instead of just listening to him rattle off bits and bobs of what he does. Dana thought that he could not wait for that phase of his life. Full of knowledge, pride for a job well done, and very tired feet, Dana headed home.

The next morning Amanda called to check in as promised. They had a wonderful chat about the evening's program, and Dana confirmed he was very happy to come in for any special events the museum may need help with, and he shared his observation of the school group in the gallery earlier in the day.

Dana was not a teacher by training, but he thought if there was room on the roster, he would like to dedicate one afternoon a month to giving tours or small presentations. Amanda was delighted to hear Dana's request. She had always hoped that a few more hours exploring the museum would encourage volunteers to take more interest in new projects or opportunities, but rarely did a volunteer take her up on the option to switch projects.

Dana was a special volunteer and Amanda knew it. She was lucky she connected with him and he had such a positive experience leading to his volunteer inquiry. Amanda explained that there were monthly volunteer get-togethers, and Dana should come and get to know the team, hear about what the museum has going on for the next month, and get some special topical training for some of the permanent galleries. She also told Dana that she would email over a complete volunteer handbook and a volunteer application. They needed to have the application on file because it had emergency contact information and other useful things for the department. The handbook was Dana's to review, make notes in, and add to as he needed.

By the end of the call Dana had confirmed his participation in the rest of the lecture series, had the next volunteer meet-up on his calendar, and was on the lookout for the application and handbook. Dana was excited he had found a way to occupy his time while the weather was cool and get to learn some new science and technology topics in the process.

LESSONS

- Volunteer recruitment can take place any time and by any person. Volunteers may meet new friends during other activities, new residents may reach out looking for ways to meet new friends, and those transitioning into a new chapter may turn to your museum to find companionship and opportunities to learn something new or expand their social network. Do not hesitate to use local media, newspapers, and radio spots as part of your recruitment strategy. Just make sure you work closely with your marketing department to ensure volunteer recruitment fits with their media calendar.
- Volunteers who engage with the public are likely the best recruiters for your volunteer program. Make sure they know about some upcoming projects and volunteer opportunities.
- Listen to casual comments about physical abilities and interests. Not only will this allow the volunteer opportunities to share a bit about themselves, but casually shared information will help any volunteer coordinator make more informed suggestions for possible volunteer roles and areas of interest in the museum.

QUESTIONS TO PONDER

1. Does your organization actively recruit volunteers, have a rolling application for volunteers, or do you have a seasonal volunteer drive to welcome new volunteers into the corps?
2. Do your volunteers know what other opportunities are available for prospective volunteers? Do they know where to direct people who ask about volunteering at the museum?
3. Do you have an open-door management style? Are volunteers able to come to you with questions, concerns, and ideas at any time?

ACCESSIBILITY CONSIDERATIONS

Physical requirements—gallery pathways/resting spots—noise/activity

- Like event volunteers, and collection volunteer projects, both explored earlier, the physical considerations for gallery and visitor engagement volunteers are a top consideration when designing accessible volunteer programs. For volunteers that spend four hours in a gallery talking to visitors, is there a chair or place for them to sit down if need be? Are there places to keep a water bottle so that they can have a drink when they need?
- When assigning gallery or program shifts, make sure that any volunteer that uses a mobility device or may need hearing or visual assistance is in spaces that are conducive to their needs and are safe for them to navigate, by touch, by sound, or with their devices.
- For volunteers presenting programs with an education collection or props, take time to speak with and train the volunteers in using the collection, manipulating the objects, and lifting or placing objects on or off carts and tables and passing them around a group of visitors. If a volunteer is uncomfortable lifting or manipulating an object, can the program continue without the object? Can the presentation be presented by a team, where one volunteer is comfortable manipulating an object while another engages with other objects? It is important for everyone's safety that volunteers know what they are handling and how to handle those objects safely, especially around visitors and program participants.

THE DIGITAL VOLUNTEER

Name: Ranya (they/them)
  Occupation: Freelance Costume Designer
  Hobbies: Movie buff, baking, spending time with friends
  Museum: Art Museum

Ranya has been a volunteer at their local art museum since their undergraduate art history class came for a special tour on impressionists' paintings their sophomore year. They were struck by the stories the tour guide shared and the exclusive collection room tour the class had that opened Ranya's imagination to all the inspiration contained in the compact storage units. As Ranya continued their academic journey, they kept finding they were drawn to the museum to seek inspiration for their assignments and spent so many hours at the museum they joined as a member and quickly became a recognized face in the galleries. One summer break Ranya reached out to volunteer with a kids camp and for each summer since they have facilitated design camps for children at the museum.

Recently Ranya accepted a position as a designer for a big production that required her to be on location for the next two years. Ranya is so excited about her new gig, and their friends at the museum could not be more proud of them as they embark on a new adventure. But there is a mutual sadness that Ranya's time at the museum is coming to an end; they have been such a fixture in the volunteer corps and will be missed.

Ranya and the museum's volunteer coordinator, Sasha, started working on a transition. Ranya had redesigned the camp course and agreed to train the next round of camp facilitators before they left. As Sasha and Ranya went through the program, Sasha casually mentioned some new acquisitions the museum was expecting before the next summer break and suggested one might be a great addition to the camp discussion. As they continued going through the lesson and the artwork in the gallery that had supported the program, Sasha had another brainstorm. With these new pieces coming into the collection and Ranya's knowledge of the museum spaces and collections, Sasha asked if Ranya might be interested in doing some virtual volunteering while they were away.

Ranya had not even considered that volunteering from afar was an option and was delighted at Sasha's suggestion. Sasha was delighted, too. The lithograph curator was begging for a volunteer to help with the digitization project, and Sasha was struggling to find a volunteer that had some knowledge of the process, an ability to recognize details, and describe the scene in a way that was helpful for the whole organization to use the collection database to plan exhibits and programs.

Ranya had helped with nearly all departments at the museum during their time on site. Sasha knew this would work out if Ranya were at all interested in lithographs. Cautiously optimistic, Sasha presented the opportunity to Ranya and suggested that before Ranya left they set up a meeting with the curator and have a chance to look at the collections so that Ranya was prepared for the digital work after they left.

Over their last couple shifts at the museum, Ranya met with the curatorial team to hear about their goals for the project, learned about the digitization process of the artwork, and how the files were stored on the museum's collection server. Ranya was confident they would be able to find time to work on part of the project while they were on set.

Ranya spent time setting up her virtual workspace on a shared drive. They set up a folder for notes on the project, a folder for the curators to drop new images and scanned copies of the paper catalog records, a folder for work in process, and a folder for completed records which the curator would use to monitor the progress of the project. Ranya had her logins to the database, the workspace, and the internal chat platform all set and ready for them by the time they walked out of the museum for the last time. An end to a life chapter Ranya thought, but excited to turn the page on the next chapter and still have a tie to their beloved museum and its collections.

The weeks passed and Ranya was busy getting preproduction tasks done as this was their busiest time of any production—meeting the actors, writers, directors, and production team, creating designs and constructing them, then making last-minute adjustments and finalizing the sets. Ranya had worked fifteen-hour days for weeks when they received a note from Sasha.

> Hi Ranya,
>
> We are all thinking of you and your grand adventure. I know you're busy setting up so I don't expect a reply soon, we just wanted to let you know we are thinking of you and can't wait to see some pictures if you can send any!
>
> I also just want to put a date on your calendar, so we don't lose track of time. We have a 30-day inactive policy for our digital logins. Could you please make sure you log in at least once for 10 minutes some time before the 26th? Let me know if there are any issues you encounter.
>
> Can't wait to catch up when your schedule settles down,
> Sasha

Ranya had not realized the days had slipped by so quickly and was grateful for Sasha's message. They took a few minutes to reply to Sasha with some fun stories about setting up shop in a remote location and also confirmed that they had logged in and refreshed their memory of the project. When the weekend came, and the crew was off for the first time since arriving, Ranya logged in and started cataloging the first piece in the "To Do" folder.

A sense of familiarity came back to Ranya, and they settled in and quickly got a couple of pieces into the collection database, connected the records to some other records in the catalog that illustrated the same themes and would make great complementary pieces for an exhibition. They followed the procedure of moving digital copies into the appropriate folders and then sent a note to Sasha and the curatorial team updating them on the work they accomplished.

As Ranya's schedule settled into a routine, they took time each week to log in to the virtual workspace and work through a few more pieces, adding the crucial data and digitized copies to the collection database, connecting the pieces to other collection items as they related to eras, subject matter, type of artwork, and making notes regarding potential programs or exhibitions in which the piece might be used. Ranya also found some pieces in interesting blog posts from art historians and linked those blog pages to the catalog record. The curatorial team was ecstatic by the work Ranya was doing, and Sasha was delighted the virtual volunteer experience was working out for the whole team. Virtual volunteering is here to stay, Sasha concluded.

LESSONS

- Having clear lines of communication, even after a volunteer has left, helps them stay connected to an organization they cared about enough to donate time and energy to. Maintain an open door to have volunteers follow their professional and personal passions while allowing them to work on projects as they fit the museum into their lives at that moment.

Chapter 8

- It is okay for a volunteer to move from one project to another, take ownership of a project and make it their own, and have them help create a succession plan if or when they move on to another project or another phase of life. Taking the time to debrief, and having succession plans with volunteers, helps the organization preserve institutional history, recognizes the volunteers as experts at the museum, and reiterates the value they have brought to the organization throughout their tenure.
- If a volunteer is switching projects, or needs to have accommodations made, taking time for them to explore their options, and working with another volunteer or staff member to learn new software, project tasks, or information will help them acclimate faster to their next project or task. Working with technology can be challenging, and knowing how to troubleshoot, where to go for help, and what steps a volunteer can fall back on to continue working on their project is important for any volunteer, especially virtual volunteers.
- Seasoned volunteers sometimes need a break; it is okay to let volunteers explore their passions. If they are committed to the organization, keeping them informed of what is going on helps them feel welcome and ready to step back into a volunteer role when their life allows for the time. Positive and ongoing communication is essential to a sustainable volunteer program.

QUESTIONS TO PONDER

1. If you are starting a virtual volunteer program, take some time to audit your on-site technology.
2. Does the project you want to do require specific software or preparation?
3. Does your staff have the expertise to develop new software or troubleshoot as needed? If the answer is no, it does not exclude your organization from developing an e-volunteer program, but staff should be trained in basic computer supervision and troubleshooting in case volunteers have questions or need help with the project.
4. Is your organization able to hand off the management of a whole project to a volunteer?

ACCESSIBILITY CONSIDERATIONS

- A volunteer does not need to be living abroad or out of the area to be a successful virtual volunteer. For many potential volunteers, the barrier of getting to the museum site could be the greatest challenge to participating. Open any virtual opportunity to volunteers near and far.
- Technology has a lot of assistance functions. When setting up a process, or implementing new software, check to see what assistance functions they

have or how well they integrate with open-source functions and programs that people rely on in other capacities (for example, assisted reading programs, image description programs, voice recognition, etc.).

The case studies presented above were intended to help you imagine how principles presented in previous chapters can be put into practice. From accessibility considerations, key objectives for certain types of volunteers and questions to ponder to help guide your policies, procedures, and actions will help you build a happy and robust volunteer team.

Appendix

ORGANIZATIONS THAT SUPPORT VOLUNTEERS
AND VOLUNTEER COORDINATORS

Below is a list of organizations that support volunteer coordinators and volunteers in nonprofit organizations. Many states have their own chapters of these organizations, and any volunteer coordinator should be encouraged to connect with them.

AL!VE—Association of Leaders in Volunteer Engagement
American Alliance of Museums
American Association for Museum Volunteers
AmeriCorps VISTA
Association of Zoo and Aquarium Docents and Volunteers
Canadian Museum Association
Council for Certification in Volunteer Administration
Directors of Volunteer Administration
International Association for Volunteer Effort
Museum Association (United Kingdom)
National Association of Interpreters
National Council of Non-profits
National Docents Symposium Council
National Park Service
Points of Light
VolunteerHub.com
VolunteerMatch.org
Volunteer Management Professionals of Canada
Volunteers of America
Work in Culture (Canada)

Or check with your local community foundations, councils, or cities for assistance.

Bibliography

American Alliance of Museums. "Museum Facts." 2014. http://www.aam-us.org/about -museums/museum-facts.

American Alliance of Museums. Center for the Future of Museums. "Museums and Society 2034: Trends and Potential Futures." December 2008. https://www.aam-us .org/wire/aam-us/museums-society-2034-trends-and-potential-futures/.

American Alliance of Museums. Center for the Future of Museums. 2021. "Museums and Equity: Volunteers." https://www.aam-us.org/2021/12/03/museums-and -equity-volunteers-2/.

American Association for Museum Volunteers (AAMV). "Standards and Best Practices for Museum Volunteer Programs." November 2011. https://aamv.org/Standards-and -Best-Practices.

The Arc. 2023. Homepage. https:///www.thearc.org.

Association of Science-Technology Centers. "2012 Science Center and Museum Statistics." 2012. http://www.astc.org/wp-content/uploads/2014/10/2012-Science -Center-Statistics.pdf.

Burger, Eric. 2021. "40 Volunteer Statistics That Will Blow Your Mind." VolunteerHub. https://volunteerhub.com/blog/40-volunteer-statistics.

Chatterjee, Helen. 2013. *Museums, Health and Well-being*. London. Ashgate Press.

DoSomething.org. "The DoSomething.org Index on Young People and Volunteering: The Year of Friends with Benefits." 2012. https://dosomething-a.akamaihd.net/sites /default/files/blog/2012-Web-Singleview_0.pdf.

Duursma, Geesje, Erwin Losekoot, and Gjalt de Jong. 2023. "The Role of Volunteers in Creating Hospitality: Insights from Museums." *Journal of Hospitality and Tourism Management* 54: 373–82.

Fidelity Charitable. 2020. "The Role of Volunteering in Philanthropy." https://www .fidelitycharitable.org/content/dam/fc-public/docs/resources/the-role-of -volunteering-in-philanthropy.pdf.

Fidelity Charitable Gift Fund. "Fidelity Charitable Gift Fund Voluteerism and Charitable Giving in 2009 Executive Summary." http://www.fidelitycharitable.org/docs /Volunteerism-Charitable-Giving-2009-Executive-Summary.pdf.

Hill Strategies. 2013. "Volunteers and Donors in Arts and Culture Organizations in Canada in 2013." https://hillstrategies.com/resource/volunteers-and-donors-in-arts -and-culture-organizations-in-canada-in-2013.

Independent Sector. 2023. "Independent Sector Releases New Value of Volunteer Time of $31.80 Per Hour." https://independentsector.org/blog/independent-sector -releases-new-value-of-volunteer-time-of-31-80-per-hour/.

Jo, S., L. Paarlberg, and R. Nesbit. 2023. "Volunteering Behaviors of People of Color in the US Communities: How Community Racial Composition Affects the Type of Organization People of Color Volunteer For." *Voluntas* 34, 760–76.

Salpeter, Miriam. 2011. "Community Service Work Increasingly Important for College Applicants." *U.S. News Money*, November 30, 2011. http://money.usnews.com/money/blogs/outside-voices-careers/2011/11/30/community-service-work-increasingly-important-for-college-applicants.

Sanburn, Josh. 2012. "Hard Labor: Inside the Mounting Backlash against Unpaid Internships." *Time*, May 21, 2012. http://content.time.com/time/magazine/article/0,9171,2114428,00.html.

Smith, Ernie. 2019. "National Volunteer Week: How Associations Are Celebrating." Associations Now. https://associationsnow.com/2019/04/national-volunteer-week-associations-celebrating/.

Thompson, Danie. 2022. "Pandemic Disrupted Labor Markets But Had Modest Impact on Retirement Timing." United States Census Bureau, September 19, 2022. https://www.census.gov/library/stories/2022/09/did-covid-19-change-retirement-timing.html.

United States Department of Labor. 2010. "Wage and Hour Division: Fact Sheet #71: Internship Programs under the Fair Labor Standards Act." April 2010. http://www.dol.gov/whd/regs/compliance/whdfs71.htm.

Weingardt, Richard. 1997. "Leadership: The World Is Run by Those Who Show Up." *Journal of Management in Engineering* 13, no. 4 (1997): 61–66.

Index

About the Authors

Kristy Van Hoven is founder of RxMuse, a consulting firm dedicated to supporting nonprofits as they embark on building health community relationships through thoughtful and sustainable partnerships. She works closely with volunteers to advocate and support the causes they are most passionate about and helps organizations align their goals to be inclusive of a range of volunteer skills and experiences. Kristy holds a PhD from the University of Leicester and is a passionate advocate for cultural education in the healthcare setting. Kristy's passion for museums and nonprofits started at an early age and has spent nearly three decades in various roles in museums across North America. Never one to sit for too long, Kristy, her husband Chris, and their pup Izzy take regular road trips to find the next great adventure and small museums along the way.

Loni Wellman is the Director of Programs for the Veterans Outreach Center in Rochester, New York. With a strong background in community outreach and volunteer management, Loni previously held the positions of Good Neighbor Program Director at Goodwill of the Finger Lakes, and Volunteer and Events Manager at the St. Augustine Lighthouse and Maritime Musuem. With a Master's Degree in Museum Studies from Johns Hopkins University and a Bachelor's degree in History from Flagler College, Loni brings a wealth of knowledge and experience from her 17 years in the nonprofit industry. Loni's dedication to service extends beyond her professional life, as she has also served 3 years as the Chair of the Rochester Area Administrators of Volunteer Services (RAAVS). Her passion for community engagement and volunteerism has resulted in impactful programs that empower volunteer coordinators. In her free time, Loni enjoys the quiet moments at home after a bustling few years, with her two pups, Mr. Oliver and Hamlet, and with her new husband, Justin.